After THIS

Understanding How Tests, Trials, and Crises Prepare You for Your Kingdom Assignment

Dr. Madelyne Douglas

AFTER THIS
Copyright © 2019 Dr. Madelyne Douglas

Published by Ear To Hear Publishing™ LLC
4741 Central St. Ste 472
Kansas City, MO 64112
www.ear2hearbooks.com

ISBN: 978-0-9861935-4-5 ▪ eBook ISBN: 978-0-9861935-5-2

Unless otherwise indicated, all Scripture quotations are taken from the New King James Version® (NKJV). Copyright © 1982 by Thomas Nelson, Inc.

Scripture quotations marked NLT are taken from the Holy Bible, New Living Translation, copyright ©1996, 2004, 2007 by Tyndale House Foundation. Used by permission of Tyndale House Publishers, Inc., Carol Stream, Illinois 60188. All rights reserved.

Scripture quotations marked NIV are taken from THE HOLY BIBLE, NEW INTERNATIONAL VERSION®, NIV® Copyright © 1973, 1978, 1984, 2011 by Biblica, Inc.® Used by permission. All rights reserved worldwide.

Scripture quotations marked TLB are taken from The Living Bible copyright © 1971 by Tyndale House Foundation. Used by permission of Tyndale House Publishers Inc., Carol Stream, Illinois 60188. All rights reserved.

Scripture quotations taken from the New American Standard Bible® (NASB), Copyright © 1960, 1962, 1963, 1968, 1971, 1972, 1973, 1975, 1977, 1995 by The Lockman Foundation Used by permission. www.Lockman.org

Scripture quotations taken from the Amplified® Bible (AMP), Copyright © 2015 by The Lockman Foundation. Used by permission. www.Lockman.org

Printed in the United States of America

Library of Congress Control Number: 2019909418

No part of this book may be reproduced or transmitted in any form or by any means, electronic or mechanical, including photocopying and recording, or by any information storage or retrieval system, except as may be expressly permitted in writing by the publisher. This book is protected by the copyright laws of the United States of America. Requests for permission should be addressed in writing to Ear To Hear Publishing™ LLC 4741 Central St. Ste 472 Kansas City, MO 64112 or visit www.eartohearbooks.com.

WHAT OTHERS WANT YOU TO KNOW ABOUT THIS BOOK...

After This is practical and an easy read for anyone who has a busy life yet needs encouragement. To the person who feels that they are in the dark and alone, to the person who feels that God doesn't see that they're in pain or has a plan for their life, I strongly recommend this book. The author is transparent about her life struggles, how she went through, and came out, and she'll remind you that you're not alone! This book encourages the reader that there is purpose in your pain and the Lord is always with you.

—Ashley Braswell
Register Nurse, Case Manager
Dallas, Texas

This book had me remembering so many emotions and inspiring memories from my own personal "night season" I experienced recently. This beautiful life manual, which is so elegantly written, will lead you in how to overcome, how to preserve, and how to stand in God's strength and not your own. Simply put, as you turn the ever so life-changing pages, you will bask in the more—more hope, more tenacity, more joy, and more endurance for your kingdom assignment ahead. If you ever needed something to get you out of your pit, you found it!

—Tammicole Bennifield,
Instructional Designer and an Intercessor
Kansas City, MO

The biblical parallels in this book clearly reinforce the truth that there is a God and that the same God who worked in the author's life situation who will work in your current circumstances. There will be life and joy after this. I truly enjoyed the read; it was easy to comprehend, digest, and apply to everyday life.

—Dr. Alisha Hill,
Exceptional Education Teacher
KCMO School District

Dedications

To those who've gone on before me and been called home by God to enjoy the beauty of the morning sun eternally...

To Larry Douglas Sr., my beloved husband of thirty-nine years. Together we endured many night seasons and enjoyed many morning sun risings and the blessing of our two beautiful children and our six grandchildren.

To Susie B. Henderson, my grandmother who took me to a little Pentecostal church where I received Jesus Christ as my personal Savior and was my example of a godly woman who shared her poetic writing abilities with me.

To Bishop Leona McGee, my first pastor and the one who recognized the call of God on my life when I was twelve. She has encouraged and taught me to guard the anointing on my life—saying it was going to bless the multitude.

To Evangelist Annie Douglas, my mother-in-law, who was my Naomi, and I was her Ruth, as she lovingly taught me how to endure the night season with grace and how to anticipate the joy that comes in the morning.

To Mother Retha Porter, who God often used as the iron that sharpened the iron in my life, never biting her tongue when necessary, yet never short of loving encouragement for me.

To Mother Mae Robinson, who believed I could "leap tall buildings in a single bound for God" and always encouraged me to "move to the front of the line for God."

To Pastor Ruby Markray, who taught me to keep a prayer in my heart, a praise on my lips, and laughter in my soul for God. She kept me in the latest fashions as my personal seamstress and taught me to sew until God called her home to enjoy the beauty of the morning sun eternally.

To Carolyn Danice Jackson, my true sister-friend and confidant who through thick and thin was always there for me along with her mother, Naomi Cobb, providing an open door for me and many others to come and rest awhile from the test and trials of the night season.

To Evangelist Earnestine Brown, my spiritual godmother, co-laborer in the Gospel, and my dear friend, who taught me practical life skills as a woman and gave me many hugs and loving words of encouragement to ease my pain during my darkest hours.

To Pastor Willa Mae Tramble, my former pastor, mentor, co-laborer in the gospel and my dear friend, who saw the call of God on my life as a young woman and allowed me to be her ministry assistant in the gospel, preparing me for the "greater works."

To Overseer Hazel Gordon, my godmother, mentor and co-laborer in the gospel who took me under her wings as a child in the church, making sure my needs were met, and showed me what it means to walk in holiness and integrity, even as a widow.

To Dorothy Carr, my guardian angel as a child, who guarded and protected me in times of trouble and spoke up for me in the church until God called her from labor to reward.

Last but certainly not least, to my dear parents, Juanita Morgan-Brown and Eliphaz Morgan Sr., who God called home while I was writing this book. They gave me life and always surrounded me with love and encouragement and allowed me to pursue my destiny in the Lord, while honoring the spiritual leadership they saw in me.

To those who remain, whose shoulders I stand upon…

To my children, Annita and Larry Jr., my anointed love gifts from God who have always shown me what true love and unwavering support looks like and who gave me the special gift of my grandchildren: Melvin, Naesion, Delvin, Larry III, Sierra, and Marshawn—true blessings to me.

To my siblings—"The Morgan Crew"—Sheila, Denise, Eliphaz, David, Catherine, Sharon, Theresa, Deleesa, Robert, Mark, Damion, J'Nai, Jessie, Latoysia, Jeffery, Yolanda, and Thaddeus, along with all of my other beloved family members who have always sincerely believed in the God in me.

To Mrs. Levera Newton, my girl scout leader, who is now 104 years old and still inspiring me to learn and to teach the lessons learned to others along this Christian journey. Thank you for everything you continue to give me.

Acknowledgments

To my pastors Keith and Latonya Tribitt and the entire Victory Temple Church Family, who are some of my greatest supporters and continue to encourage me that in Christ "the sky is the limit."

To the Intercessory Prayer Team—Joann Glenn, Garry and Chavos Buycks, James and Angel Byrd, Evelyn Hill, Celeste Barton, Delores Washington, Duane Washington, Aretha Bryant, Gina Tusa, Angela Donahue, Greta Smith, Victoria Jackson, Antonio Jackson, Desmond Turner, Dixie Jones, and many others who pushed in prayer for me from the inception to the birthing of this book.

To Minister Terrance Smith, Bertha Reese, and Yahna Gibson—who sent me special words of encouragement, along with the scriptures each day that brightened my way and helped me to focus on God's goodness and mercy while writing this book, even in the midst of my "night season."

To John Hudson—who was a driving force behind me, not only insisting that I write this book, but also making sure I completed it, assuring me that there are many more books in me and encouraging me to stay the course.

To Yahna Gibson—for your editorial support, for always being my sounding board in times of need, and for pushing me through some of the toughest seasons of my life with your joy and laughter.

To Chavos Buycks—for your editorial support and encouragement in seeing this book come to life.

To Ear To Hear Publishing, LLC—for your creativity and artistry in the cover layout and sheer tenacity in publishing this book.

Contents

Foreword xiii
Introduction 1

1. The Night Season 7
2. Job's Night Season 19
3. What the Old Saints Knew 31
4. My Personal Night Season 39
5. He Restoreth My Soul 61
6. An Avalanche in the Valley 67
7. God Has a Master Plan 81
8. After This 105

Epilogue 111
About the Author 117

Foreword

I've been given the awesome responsibility of writing the foreword for Dr. Madelyne Douglas's inaugural book, After This. I've been contemplating what to write because I wanted to get it just right, so I reflected on our many conversations. One topic in particular stands out—transparency! Transparency is defined as clarity, openness, straightforwardness, candor and, amazingly, the word accountability popped up. All of the words resonated with me, particularly accountability.

When I think about our Christian walk, I recognize that, in our flesh, we often forget that we are accountable to each other. In that accountability, we must understand that our journey is not just for ourselves. We are accountable and responsible to each other to be transparent—open, clear, and straightforward. That's what you will find in After This, a raw, candid, often heart-wrenching truth; a truth that reminds us that in our darkest hours God is with us.

Dr. D. impresses this truth upon us through her life story and the stories of both Job and Joseph. She reminds us that God knows the plans He has for us (Jeremiah 29:11), and He is preparing us for the next leg of our journey or, as she so eloquently puts it, "our kingdom assignment." We have to trust Him and continue to walk upright before Him, even when the pain is unbearable. As Dr. D. says, "life goes on and, no matter what we go through, God is always with us. That's His promise."

As you delve into this book, remember that even though you might be in a season that is unfamiliar to you, after this your healing will begin. His promises await you. You CAN and WILL make it through your "season of preparation."

Be blessed!

Yahna Gibson

Former President and CEO of Habitat for Humanity, Kansas City; Teacher; and Inspirational Motivator

Introduction

Butterflies are very interesting creatures to me. Each time I see a butterfly in all its splendor and beauty flying about for the entire world to see and admire, I'm reminded of the process it took for the butterfly to become such a beautiful specimen. When my son was in junior high school he had to do a project that demonstrated the step-by-step process, or metamorphosis, that a butterfly goes through from conception to full maturity before becoming the majestic creation that it is. I was amazed at its growth and development process.

For a butterfly to grow into a mature adult, it must go through four stages of development: egg, larva, pupa, and adult. Each stage has a different purpose. In the first sage the butterfly egg is usually laid on the leaf of a plant that camouflages and protects it from any predator looking to consume it before its full development. In the second stage the egg finally hatches, and what emerges from the egg is not a beautiful butterfly, as one might imagine, but rather

After This

a partially developed mass of matter called larva, otherwise known as a caterpillar. At first glance one might wonder how anything of beauty could come from this slimy little creature.

The butterfly does not stay in the caterpillar stage for very long. In the larva stage the caterpillar mostly eats from its protective plant and grows rapidly. As the caterpillar grows, an outer shell grows and covers its tiny body. In order for the caterpillar to stretch out and grow to its full length, it must shed this outer shell. The third stage is called the pupa stage. As soon as the caterpillar is done growing and has reached its full length and weight, it forms itself into a pupa or sack also known as chrysalis. At first glance from the outside of the pupa, it looks as if the caterpillar is just resting. But not so!

Deep inside the dark center of the pupa, a complete transformation is taking place in the life of the caterpillar. Inside the pupa the old body parts of the caterpillar are experiencing a remarkable transformation called "metamorphosis," changing from one stage to another to become the beautiful butterfly that will emerge. The tissue, limbs, and organs of the caterpillar have all been changed as the transformation inside the pupa is being finished and is now ready for the final stage of the butterfly's maturing cycle.

It is said that some who have witnessed this stage of the butterfly's transformation can actually see the butterfly with all its beautiful colors as it grows larger and larger inside the tiny pupa sack. And because the butterfly appears to be struggling and full grown inside the tiny sack, a person prematurely cuts open the sack to set the butterfly free of its tiny cocoon, thinking he is freeing the butterfly from its struggle. The person finds out later that he actually hurt the butterfly by interrupting the development process. The consequence of this interruption is that the butterfly dies and never fulfills its purpose.

Introduction

The fourth and final stage is when the caterpillar has completed its transformation process inside the pupa sack and becomes a mature adult butterfly, ready to emerge. Much like the beautiful butterfly, we as God's greatest creation must also go through a season of transformation (a metamorphosis) from a state of spiritual immaturity to a state of spiritual maturity as God prepares us for our kingdom assignment. Too often we try to fly before our wings have been developed. We resist the process of development, never becoming fully equipped to operate effectively in our kingdom assignment. Sometimes someone sees your gifts and talents and gets overly excited about what they outwardly see in you, not realizing you have not been fully developed and they prematurely set you free from God's process, only to later see you make a crash landing because of your inability to fly. God desires for us to be mature and fly high in our calling. And the process of development that the Lord uses to mature and transform the life of a believer is a night season like the pupa sack for the caterpillar.

In this book you will journey with three main characters, Job, Joseph and yours truly, as you experience the step-by-step development process to maturity in preparation for your kingdom assignment. All three main characters have been chosen by God, but they needed to be equipped through a night season.

First, Job helps us understand what going through great tests and trials looks like, while getting to know God on a much greater level. You will also see how his support team erred in their role and his response to them.

Second, I share my night seasons with a vulnerable heart. Some of the test and trials I experienced were not always readily understood, and at times I even wondered why me? But like the butterfly, they prepared me to fly. I share how not to get stuck and keep moving, and how to handle your emotions in crisis by understanding the I-WAR cycle. I challenge you to examine the fruit of the Spirit in your life and ask yourself where are you growing or not growing.

Lastly, Joseph will show you that even though God gives you a vision or a dream and even reveals to you the future of what things will look like in your life, there is still a process you must go through before getting to your kingdom assignment. I also explain the five levels you need to go through to get to that kingdom assignment.

I wrote this book and titled it After This because I counsel many people who are in a crisis and saw a need to help give understanding and be an encouraging light in the night season. See this book as your one-on-one counseling session in your night season. The night season can be a difficult process as God hammers out the details and unfolds His purpose for your life. Sometimes what God has assigned for you to do in the kingdom is so strategic and vital that only God knows the depth of what it will take to prepare you for this special assignment. Therefore, the magnitude of this assignment has to be slowly revealed, even to you, in a manner you can humbly handle as God prepares to reveal and work His glorious plan through you.

My desire is for you to see your night season as a necessary requirement for you to be prepared to fully walk in your kingdom assignment and for you to know that what you are facing now will work for your good. How can I write this with such surety? Because God promised us in Romans 8:28 (AMPC, emphasis added) "We are assured and know that… all things work together and are [fitting into a plan] for good to and for those who love God and are called according to [His] design and purpose."

Introduction

I want to inspire those who feel hopeless after experiencing what may seem to be unbearable circumstances in their lives. In the night season the enemy whispers discouragement, "This is it. It will always be like this." And he sprinkles doubt in your heart, "You should just let go of your faith and abort your God-ordained purpose." The enemy may even declare, "What God is producing in you will never come to pass." But he's a liar. Be encouraged by the words of David the psalmist.

Weeping may endure for a [night season] but [after this] joy comes in the morning.
Psalm 30:5b, AMP

Although you may not be able to fully understand all you are going through during this night season of testing and preparation, if you will just hold on until the morning—God's appointed time for your breakthrough—everything will be alright; I'm living proof. And when your season of preparation is over, you will be fully equipped for your next kingdom assignment.

Chapter One

The Night Season

To every thing there is a season, and a time to every purpose under the heaven.

—*Ecclesiastes 3:1*

The night season is a time in your life when God allows His chosen vessels to experience great tests and trials while being equipped in the school of preparation. The purpose of this preparation is to get you ready for your kingdom assignment.

The night season of preparation is different for every individual, in accordance with your unique ability, call, and assignment from God. The intensity of each person's test differs according to their individual assignment. God knows how much we are able to bear and the kingdom responsibility each of us can handle. Our individual lesson plans from God in preparation for our kingdom assignments can look drastically different.

After This

Let's examine Matthew 25:14-15:

For the kingdom of heaven is like a man traveling to a far country, who called his own servants and delivered his goods to them. And to one he gave five talents, to another two, and to another one, to each according to his own ability; and immediately he went on a journey.

In this scripture we see God's wisdom and plan as He gives out talents (the inner ability to accomplish your God-given assignments) to His servants, each according to their individual ability. To one He gave five talents, to another two, and to another only one. This diverse distribution level of the talents didn't mean that anyone was greater or better than the other in God's eyes. God knows each of our strengths and abilities, and He individually distributes our assignments accordingly to equip us for our own unique kingdom assignments.

The method used to transport each of us through the night season of preparation can come in many forms. The method God used to test the children of Israel was a wilderness journey on their way to the Promised Land. The journey should have only taken them eleven days to complete, but because of pride, murmuring, disobedience, and unbelief, many of them failed their test and died in the wilderness, never seeing the Promised Land. Notice how the scripture describes the purpose of their journey:

Remember how the LORD your God led you all the way in the wilderness these forty years, to humble and test you in order to know what was in your heart, whether or not you would keep his commands.

Deuteronomy 8:2, NIV

The Night Season

The wilderness (their night season of testing) was the vehicle used to try their faith, test their humility, reveal their true hearts for God, and prove whether or not they would keep His commands.

Some of you may experience your vehicle of testing as an attack on your health, adversity on your job, a family crisis with various attacks against your family members, loss of a job, the death of a loved one, incarceration, homelessness, substance addiction, or abuse and recovery. Some of you may experience the mode of transportation as challenges in school, marital problems, separation, divorce, financial crises, physical abuse, emotional abuse, sexual abuse, neglect, mental health issues, personal identity crisis, and sadly, some through church hurts and disappointments.

Whatever the circumstance, remember God knows what you are able to bear and what it takes to prove and prepare you to be a vessel of honor ready for the Master's use.

Also remember that the more talents (responsibilities) you receive, the more will be required of you. Therefore, more testing and trials (wisdom classes) in the school of preparation will be required to equip you for a higher level in your kingdom assignment.

> *For everyone to whom much is given, from him much will be required; and to whom much has been committed, of him they will ask the more.*
> *Luke 12:48b*

As a chosen vessel of God, the higher your call, the more humble you must be. You cannot be seen as one who blows his or her own trumpet and wants to be up front in the spotlight of men, but rather as one who knows the awesome responsibility associated with being handpicked by God to do the Master's will. Notice how God makes His selections in this next scripture:

> *For the eyes of the Lord search back and forth across the whole earth, looking for people whose hearts are perfect [willing] toward him, so that he can show his great power in helping them.*
>
> 2 Chronicles 16:9, TLB

The Bible declares that the Lord Himself searches the whole earth looking specifically for those chosen vessels who have a heart (love) toward Him. And He strengthens and prepares them to show Himself strong through them. This doesn't mean that these chosen individuals will be without human weaknesses; it means that even with human frailties they love the Lord and are willing to obey. These individuals have accepted Jesus Christ as their personal Savior and have a sincere desire to surrender their self-centered will to do God's will in their lives and give Him all the glory.

God lovingly uses the circumstances of our lives (good or bad) to accomplish His purpose, because He knows what it will take to mature every chosen vessel. This may mean allowing Satan permission to try us as he did with his faithful servant Job when Satan unleashed all manner of evil upon Job to test him.

> *God will use whatever it takes to shake us, mold us, and make us into prepared vessels fit for His use.*

God can also use the circumstances of our lives that we get ourselves into, as He did with King David when he willingly sinned with Bathsheba, wreaking all manner of havoc upon his own life. God will use whatever it takes to shake us, mold us, and make us into prepared vessels fit for His use.

This shaking, molding, and pruning process is not an easy procedure because it requires us as earthen vessels to surrender to the will of the potter, which has proven to be one of man's most difficult tasks and a primary reason some people's season of testing lasts much longer than others'. For every chosen vessel to get through their seasons of growth effectively, they must make a conscious decision to let go of their personal steering wheels and let Jesus Christ take the wheel. We must trust that the one who made us knows what it takes to prepare us for the greater work.

Developing Our Fruit

Again, God knows what each of us is able to bear, so don't be discouraged or give up. Remember, God's goal is not to destroy you, but to develop you as a vessel fit in every area to fulfill your kingdom assignment. The way we behave as Christians doing the work of ministry is very important because we represent Jesus Christ to others. Therefore, as a vital part of our character-building process, God wants to begin by developing the nine essential areas in our lives known as the fruit of the Spirit. Let's examine our fruit:

> *But the fruit of the Spirit is love, joy, peace, longsuffering, gentleness, goodness, faith, meekness, temperance: against such there is no law.*
> *Galatians 5:22-23, KJV*

Love (agape love) is unselfish godly love that causes one to give of oneself freely without asking anything in return and without considering the condition of the person to which it's given. Many have fallen short in this area because most humans seem to be wired to always expect something in return for what they give, and when it's not received, they find themselves selfishly withholding their love, not realizing that the fruit of love is a vital part of their kingdom assignments.

Joy is deeper than mere emotional happiness that lasts only for a while or is dependent upon present circumstances. Godly joy is a lasting inward strength rooted in the awareness that God is always with us, regardless of the circumstance (Psalm 28:7). Joy is essential to our maturity and growth because it gives us the strength to push through every obstacle that comes into our lives.

Peace is more than the absence of conflict. It's the calm state of a soul resting and trusting in the promises of God (John 14:27). Peace is developed by trusting God's plan for our lives and being confident that He who has begun a good work in us will complete it until the day of His return (Philippians 1:6).

Longsuffering is the ability to endure patiently, show tolerance with others, and have a willingness to forgive, even when wronged (Ephesians 4:2). Wow! Many of us know that this is an area that the Lord has to perfect within us. Longsuffering is vital to your kingdom assignment, especially when working with hurting people. Remember, if we're not developed in this area, "hurt people always hurt people."

Gentleness is goodness in action, sweetness of disposition, tenderness when dealing with others, and being compassionate, kind, and friendly (Ephesians 4:32). Gentleness must be the shining light in your life that will help draw this generation to Christ. It is simply being nice to be nice, which is a very difficult task for many. Therefore, your gentleness must be developed.

Goodness is moral excellence and virtue in the life of an individual (Colossians 3:12—14). With this moral excellence you will be a shining example and living proof of a Christ-life that will draw others to the Lord.

Faith is complete trust and confidence in God's ability with the assurance that He is going to accomplish His purpose in your life, regardless of the situation. Without this confident trust in God, it is impossible to please Him or to accomplish your kingdom assignment (Hebrews 11:1–6).

Meekness is not weakness or the absence of power. It is an inward power under the control of the Almighty in our lives (1 Peter 3:4). With meekness operating in your life, you will learn that you have nothing to prove to man concerning who you are in Christ. Rather you simply learn to confidently walk in your God-strength while drawing others to the Lord.

Temperance is self-control with the ability to control your thoughts, words, and actions from a place of inward peace, regardless of the circumstances (2 Peter 1:5–9). Here again is an area that God will spend a lot of time developing in our lives. Many who don't have temperance operate under the spirit of control, which means they want to control others, but have not mastered the art of controlling themselves.

The Pruning Process

In the natural, pruning means to cut off or trim back parts that hinder growth. In the spiritual, God allows situations in our lives to cut away the dead and overgrown parts that hinder our new growth in the Lord. Through this pruning process, God's goal is to produce more fruit in our lives. Hear what the Lord says in this scripture:

> *I am the true vine, and my Father is the gardener. He cuts off every branch in me that bears no fruit, while every branch that does bear fruit he prunes so that it will be even more fruitful. I am the vine; you are the*

branches. If you remain in me and I in you, you will bear much fruit; apart from me you can do nothing.
John 15:1-2, 5, NIV

This pruning process is not always easy because the enemy comes to try you in every area of your Christian walk to stop your fruit from being fully developed. Peter says it like this:

Beloved, think it not strange concerning the fiery trial which is to try you, as though some strange thing happened unto you.
1 Peter 4:12, KJV

The areas to guard during the pruning include: your faithfulness to the will of God, your love for others, your peace of mind, your internal and external attitudes, your motives, your humility, your gifts, your ability to forgive, and most of all your joy, because that's where your strength lies.

God's preferred pruning tool is the Word of God.

The Word of God is sharp, and it will cut, pierce, and divide between the soul and spirit, the joints and the marrow (Hebrews 4:12). This means the Word of God has the power to discern what's in our hearts, and it's sharp enough to prune us without destroying the good parts of our lives, which God desires to use.

Why Do I Need to Go Through This Process?

Some do not heed the Word alone, so God uses any means necessary to get us ready. Others are not fully committed to God and only partially obey His commandments. Many have allowed the ungodly ways of the world (works of the flesh) to invade their hearts through the unguarded gates (ears, eyes, mouth, nose, or personal body parts) of their lives. Therefore, Satan has entered through damaging thoughts, words, ungodly acts, things, people, and impurities despite what we know is in opposition to the Word of God or against our moral consciousness. According to the Word of God, these works of the flesh can hinder us from inheriting the kingdom of God. Let's examine the works of the flesh according to the Scriptures:

> *Now the works of the flesh are evident, which are: adultery, fornication, uncleanness, lewdness, idolatry, sorcery, hatred, contentions, jealousies, outbursts of wrath, selfish ambitions, dissensions, heresies, envy, murders, drunkenness, revelries, and the like; of which I tell you beforehand, just as I also told you in time past, that those who practice such things will not inherit the kingdom of God.*
> *Galatians 5: 19–21*

Make no mistake about it; these works of the flesh (impurities) can damage us as believers, even while we are in the hands of the potter (Jeremiah 18:4).

God the potter sees the marred cracks in our lives, and He wants to make us over again in accordance with His will as He prepares us for the greater work. For Jesus declared in His Word that if we believe in Him, we would not only do the works that He did, but we would do even greater works in the kingdom (John 14:12).

The main reason for the pruning process is simply that the church (God's called-out body of believers) is not fully equipped to handle this next level of God's kingdom assignments. I know that some may feel that the level of anointing you received from God many years ago with all of your past victories in ministry is sufficient to qualify you for this next level of kingdom ministry. However, God is saying it is not sufficient for this next level of ministry. The former season of anointing represents where God was, and now God wants to sufficiently anoint you for where He is.

Fresh Oil Comes After the Pruning

After God prunes us, He pours upon us the fresh oil of anointing with new strategy and greater power from on high. He wants to stir up the gifts within us and empower us for the greater work of setting souls free from every form of bondage.

There is a shift occurring in the kingdom of God. Fresh oil is being poured on the willing heart, and the cloud of glory (God's divine presence) is moving to the next dispensation of time and kingdom ministry! Therefore, all those who want to hold onto yesterday's anointing, past victories, and former traditions in ministry, which were wonderful in their season, will miss the joy and privilege of the fresh anointing and present move of God. To be a part of this shift, you must move with the cloud and declare like David, "I shall be anointed with fresh oil" (Psalm 92:10b, KJV).

> "A fresh anointing will prepare you to be used by God in a whole new dimension..."

A fresh anointing will prepare you to be used by God in a whole new dimension to impact a whole new generation for God. This new dimension of ministry requires God's chosen vessel to be tried and tested in God's refining fire, as He transforms you into a strong and resilient vessel, fit for His use.

The Night Season

Quality Tested for the Master's Use

My daughter works for a company that makes plastic food containers, which go through an intense testing process to check for accuracy, quality, durability, and safety before being stamped with the company's seal of approval. This seal of approval signifies that the product bearing the company name is safe and ready to be distributed to the public for human usefulness. Now just think, if man will not allow just anything to be sent out to the public for human use, what about God? He too has a standard of excellence before stamping His seal of approval upon each of us. His seal of approval signifies that each of His chosen vessels have been quality tested for accuracy (truthfulness), quality (excellence), durability (strength), and safety (Spirit-filled), before being released to represent Him in effective ministry.

The night season of preparation is an intense process because it can be a very dark, lonely, and difficult season. But please know that even as God was with the three Hebrew boys when they were being quality tested and tried in the fiery furnace (see Daniel 3), He will also be with you. And after this, you will come forth equipped and ready for your next kingdom assignment, and no one will even detect the smell of God's refining smoke on you.

Chapter Two

Job's Night Season

May the day of my birth perish, and the night that said, "A boy is conceived!"

—*Job 3:3, NIV*

There are many examples in the Word of God of individuals who went through a night season. However, Job stands out as a classic example of one who went through a very difficult season of tests and trials.

Job was a wealthy man living in a land called Uz (it roughly correlates to the current land of Jordan) with his large family and extensive flocks. He was blameless and upright always being careful to do what was right and avoid doing evil (Job 1:1). Then one day along came Satan (the adversary and accuser) appearing before the Lord. Then God, who knew the heart of His servant Job, boasted to Satan about Job's goodness and faithfulness. Satan contended with God, accused Job of only being good and faithful because God had abundantly blessed him with riches and earthly possessions (Job 1:7–12).

Also Satan knew that God had put a protective hedge all around Job and his family. Satan asked God for permission to test Job's faithfulness with various trials and tribulations. The enemy declared that without God's hedge of protection, Job would curse God to His face. God granted the enemy's request and removed the protective hedge. And just like that, without any input from Job, his night season began. God allowed Job to be tested in every way. However, there was one exception, Satan was forbidden to personally touch Job in the process.

Wow! Have you ever wondered what kind of conversation the Lord has had with Satan about you? Have you ever wondered how much Satan hates your faithfulness toward God and his desire to test you? Have you ever wondered if God will accept Satan's challenge and allow you to be tested, seemingly beyond measure to prove your God strength and steadfast faithfulness toward him? Well, strap on your boots and wonder no more because it will happen if you're one of God's chosen vessels, anointed for the greater works and called to show forth His glory in the earth.

God will not only use these times of testing to show forth your God strength to Satan, but God will also use these tests and trials to show you your own areas of weakness and your great need for Him as your Savior. Job's test was precisely designed for his personal making. God has personally designed each of our tests according to what He knows will specifically prepare us to be used by Him.

Job's Night Season

Plunged Into the Night Season

Sometimes, much like Job, without warning we are plunged headfirst into a night season of testing and trials. One of Satan's greatest tactical moves is to initially stun you by hitting you so fast and hard that you don't know who or what hit you. His mission is for you to quickly retreat, give up, and faint with discouragement during the first round of the battle. He swiftly jabs you with the disbelief and shock of what you've been plunged into. However, God has told us in His Word not to be surprised by any of these things that come to test us. Instead, He has commanded us to use our weapon of praise and to rejoice because we are participants of Christ's suffering (1 Peter 4:12–13).

Job was hit hard and fast! In the course of one day, Job received four devastating messages, each one bearing news that his livestock, servants, and ten children had all died due to an attack of reckless invaders and natural catastrophes. The blow was so massive that it sent Job to his knees. Yet despite his painful circumstances, Job found inner strength to pull out his weapon of praise and bless the Lord. Listen as Job speaks:

> "Job found inner strength to pull out his weapon of praise and bless the Lord."

> *Naked came I out of my mother's womb, and naked shall I return thither: the LORD gave, and the LORD hath taken away; blessed be the name of the LORD. In all this Job sinned not, nor charged God foolishly.*
> *Job 1:21, KJV*

During a test is not the time to blame God. It's not the time to get angry. It's not the time to make excuses to quit or to sin. But it is a time to draw close to the Lord and be still, knowing that He is God, and He is with you (Psalm 46:10). It is here that we learn to trust God like we've never trusted Him before. Again, this will require you to surrender your carnal will and truly trust the Lord's plan for your life. So let go and give God the wheel and let Him navigate you through this season. Regardless of what it looks like, know that God is with you and everything will be alright and will eventually work out for your good. Even when your human emotions want to challenge God and try to make you throw in the towel, meditate on this scripture:

> *For I know the plans and thoughts that I have for you, says the LORD, plans for peace and well-being and not for disaster, to give you a future and a hope.*
> *Jeremiah 29:11, AMP*

Satan Is a Relentless Opponent

Satan is ruthless and couldn't care less about your feelings or your pain. He is determined to knock you out of the race and accuse you of being a loser or unfaithful before God. His ultimate goal is to prove God wrong concerning His choice to save and use mankind, making it of no effect. Satan is not easily swayed concerning his goal, which is to steal, to kill and to destroy your purpose (John 10:10). Therefore, he will continue to try and wear you down to the bitter end.

However, God's end goal in all of this is to give us life and that more abundantly. So know that He is with you in the battle, and He will not let you perish. In this spiritual battle the Lord always knows when it is time to ring the bell and pull you out of the ring and give you rest from the battle. Satan is under God's authority, and when commanded, he must periodically pause from his evil tactics during this season, as God allows us time to recover.

However, be aware, Satan will return. He's waiting for the opportunity to try and ultimately defeat you, but remember, you are victorious in God. The Lord knows how much you can endure and will not allow more to be put upon you than you're able to bear.

> *No temptation has overtaken you except such as is common to man; but God is faithful, who will not allow you to be tempted beyond what you are able, but with the temptation will also make the way of escape, that you may be able to bear it.*
> *1 Corinthians 10:13*

Satan Returned for More

Satan appeared before God a second time, and God allowed him another chance to test Job. God granted Satan permission to touch Job personally, but restricted him from taking Job's life. Job was afflicted with horrible boils (Job 2:4–7). His wife was so distraught that she encouraged him to give up, curse God, and die, but Job refused. Job replied to his wife in her distress:

> *You talk like a foolish woman. Should we accept only good things from the hand of God and never anything bad? So in all this, Job said nothing wrong.*
> *Job 2:10, NLT*

The test and trials that we go through in our night season of preparation are very real. They can affect us in ways we could never imagine. Our own human emotions, as well as the emotions of those closest to us, can be all over the place. I often think of how Mrs. Job must have been feeling emotionally, reminding myself that these were her children, servants and possessions that were destroyed, as well as Job's. Oh, the pain, suffering, and loss she too endured, while she watched her husband live in tremendous pain and didn't understand what was going on.

During your night season of testing, those closest to you may not have the same spiritual strength, understanding, and fortitude as you do, therefore, they may speak foolishly out of their own pain or because they do not want to see you suffering. This emotional pain can be against God or against you as the one who seems to be willing to trust God and endure. It can even be against the whole process concerning what you're going through. Your decision to remain steadfast may cause them to believe you have lost your mind. They will speak from their flesh and tell you to give up and may even tell you to go ahead and curse God and die. Please understand that in the times of crisis, especially those orchestrated by Satan, one of his old familiar tactics is to start a war in your inner circle. However, notice what this scripture tell us:

> *For we wrestle not against flesh and blood, but against principalities, against powers, against the rulers of the darkness of this world, against spiritual wickedness in high places.*
> *Ephesians 6:12, KJV*

Satan's strategy is to have you so focused on striking out at one another, especially those closest to you, that you take your eyes off Jesus, which is one of Satan's cunning war maneuvers. You must be aware that this battle is not against flesh and blood, which includes your spouse, your children, your family members, your friends, your pastor, your church members, your boss, your coworkers, your neighbors, or anyone else. But this battle is against Satan and his host, who will use anything and anybody to attack you during your night season of being tested and prepared by God.

Special Note:

Husbands and wives please be aware that during these times of testing, the enemy will try to emotionally or even physically divide you, but stay strong and stay together in the name of Jesus Christ! Even if you don't fully understand the test, you must continue to trust God and His plan for your life. Cover each other in prayer, and guard your emotions and your intimacy both naturally and spiritually. Keep your positive lines of communication open and loving with each other. And remember that your best supporter should be the one closest to you.

The Support Team

As Job's night season of testing raged on, Job's three closest friends and confidants, Eliphaz, Bildad, and Zophar came with good intentions to support him in his season of pain by sitting and mourning in silent grief with him for seven days. Sometimes all a person initially needs is to know that their support team is there. On the seventh day Job finally broke his silence, and his words seemed to confuse, frustrate, and even anger his three friends. One by one each shared his own fleshly opinions concerning the reason for Job's affliction, which proved to be devastating (Job 4:4–31).

How painfully discouraged Job was to hear those that he'd depended on for a prayer covering and support accuse him of sinful actions. How hurtful to be called a liar and to see the blame placed on his children for the reason God brought these terrible things upon him. How devastating to hear that he'd gotten what he'd deserved from God for his sinful ways. Job was irritated and responded to his friends' discouraging remarks:

> *You, however, smear me with lies; you are worthless physicians, all of you!*
>
> *Job 13:4, NIV*

Job viewed his support team as worthless. Please remember that the fleshly opinions spoken from the mouth of a friend who is supposed to be supportive during a crisis period can be devastating.

Support Team Be Aware

During the season of testing and trials, the support team must be very prayerful and in tune with God. The team must seek God for wisdom as to how to be supportive to the brother or sister who's being tested and prepared. Sometimes the best support we can give is to be a good listening ear. In the Garden of Gethsemane when Jesus was going through the agony of preparing to die on the cross (His night season), all He needed from His support team (the disciples) was to pray and watch with Him, not human reasoning as to why He was going through this night season. Hear what Jesus said in this scripture:

Job's Night Season

My soul is overwhelmed with sorrow to the point of death. Stay here and keep watch with me.

Matthew 26:38, NIV

It's very important that those who've been assigned as members of the support team understand the importance of their role as supporters. Although Jesus knew that His disciples may not have understood all that He was going through and that they could only go so far with Him during His night season, all He needed was their support. He needed them to cover Him in prayer as He faced His overwhelming kingdom assignment of dying to save mankind. How discouraging for Jesus to find His support team sleeping during the time He desperately needed them the most.

Going a little farther, he fell with his face to the ground and prayed, "My Father, if it is possible, may this cup [death] be taken from me. Yet not as I will, but as you will." Then he returned to the disciples and found them sleeping. "Couldn't you men keep watch with me for one hour?" he asked Peter.

Matthew 26:39–40, NIV

Jesus was simply asking them to be alert, emotionally present, and supportive during His darkest hour. As members of the support team we must be very aware of the danger of operating in the flesh (self-driven behavior) when working with those God has assigned us to cover in prayer and support. Job's friends started out with good intentions to support him through his night season. However, after supporting Job so far and not fully understanding God's master plan of preparation for Job's life, they strayed from their supportive role (assignment) to the unsupportive position of analyzing Job's situation in their flesh.

Eliphaz, Bildad, and Zophar allowed their fleshly assumptions to move them out of their assigned roles as supporters. What a battle for Job to be in combat with Satan and his support team too. This round of the battle produced much discouragement in Job, and we see him sinking into the dark depth of despair, which caused him to become sarcastic, impatient, hopeless, and afraid. Job's night season uncovered many areas for improvement. Job had the opportunity to take a good look at himself as his human emotions and inner weaknesses began to surface.

> Job's night season uncovered many areas for improvement.

His human emotions were all over the place, so much so that he had to repent before God for allowing the pain and suffering of his flesh to speak. He was ignorant to what the Lord was really doing in his life. Listen to Job's repentant heart:

> *I know that you can do anything, and no one can stop you. You asked, "Who is this that questions my wisdom with such ignorance?" It is I—and I was talking about things I knew nothing about, things far too wonderful for me to understand. You said, "Listen and I will speak! I have some questions for you, and you must answer them." I had only heard about you before, but now I have seen you with my own eyes. I take back everything I said, and I sit in dust and ashes to show my repentance.*
>
> *Job 42:2–6, NLT*

Does any of this sound familiar to those of you who've ever endured a night season of being tried in afflicting fire?

This is the kind of fire that tests every human emotion you were able to bear. Fire that caused you to see your own human weaknesses and to realize your need and dependency on God as your only source. This fire is none other than the refining fire of God. The fire that comes to purify, strengthen, and prepare you with abundant power and ability for your kingdom assignment.

Hear the praise of the psalmist after much affliction:

For You have tried us, O God; You have refined us as silver is refined. You brought us into the net; You laid an oppressive burden upon our loins. You made men ride over our heads; we went through fire and through water, yet You brought us out into a place of abundance.
Psalm 66:10–12, NASB

A Place of Abundance

Job endured much, but remember to whom much is given, much is required. Job came out of his night season into a place of abundance with a double portion of blessings and most of all a greater knowledge of the character of God. Up until this point Job had only heard about God with no understanding of who God really was (Job 42:5). But after coming out of the night season, Job knew who God was up close and personal, and he was ready to do exploits for the Lord. Hear what God promises those who get to know Him:

But the people that do know their God shall be strong, and do exploits [mighty acts].
Daniel 11:32b, KJV

In this next season only those who know God (not solely based on what others say), spend time in His presence, and enter the classroom of preparation will experience the joy of doing exploits for God. Job endured the process, and God abundantly blessed him as a result of it.

> *The LORD blessed the latter part of Job's life more than the former part.*
>
> *Job 42:12a, NIV*

Like Job, you too will be abundantly blessed after enduring the tests and trials of your night season, and your latter season will be greater. Although you may not fully understand God's ultimate plan in the beginning of your night season and may even question the process, please know that after this, all that you have endured is going to work for your good, according to God's purpose for your life.

> *And we know that all things work together for good to those who love God, to those who are the called according to His purpose.*
>
> *Romans 8:28*

Remember that while going through the testing and trials of your night season you may walk through periods of discouragement, hurt, or even be shamed by the ignorance of man, just as Job endured. However, God promises this in His Word:

> *Instead of your shame you will receive a double portion, and instead of disgrace you will rejoice in your inheritance. And so you will inherit a double portion in your land, and everlasting joy will be yours.*
>
> *Isaiah 61:7, NIV*

Chapter Three

What the Old Saints Knew

*I will bless the L*ORD *at all times: his praise shall continually be in my mouth.*

—Psalm 34:1, KJV

When I was a young girl, I used to hear the old saints (which we so fondly called the mature, saved members of the church) sing many songs. At the time I had no idea what the words to those songs really meant. I never fully understood why these old gospel songs always made the old saints rejoice and joyously lift their heads. The old saints drew strength as they praised God for His goodness and mercy toward them, despite the difficulty of their night seasons.

This always puzzled me, especially in light of the fact that I knew firsthand the difficult times many of the old saints were experiencing. Although I didn't always understand the meaning of the words of the songs, the excitement and encouragement that was generated as they sang before the Lord was contagious! It was like sparks of fire jumping from one side to the other until the whole congregation caught on fire with the Holy Spirit, who fell in the midst of their praise. These old saints steadfastly believed that the joy of the Lord was their strength (Nehemiah 8:10). This kind of joy gave them strength to conquer anything.

> **These old saints steadfastly believed that the joy of the Lord was their strength.**

There were many of those old songs that seemed to spark the fire of determination during their night season, but there were three songs that always stuck in my head as a child:
- "We'll Understand It Better By and By"
- "Trouble Don't Last Always"
- "Something Inside of Me Is Telling Me to Go Ahead"

Oh, How They Praised God On Those Old Gospel Songs!

I particularly remember my grandmother, who was very graceful and a sharp dresser. She was normally so cool, calm, and collected in her demeanor, until one day at church she showed a different side. I knew she was going through a night season of testing, but when she heard the words of those old gospel songs being sung with such passion, she lost her cool. I watched my grandmother praise the Lord until she danced out of her fancy shoes and her fine hat went flying off her head. Tears of joy streamed down her face and collected beneath her chin and dripped down the front of her beautiful brocade dress. I tried fanning her to calm her down like

I saw the ushers do with the others who were caught up in high praise (the kind of praise that summons help from the sanctuary of God). But her praise was so real and infectious I felt like I was on fire with whatever it was my grandmother felt. I wondered in my young mind, "What is this?"

At times I'd heard them shout out words to one another such as: "Go ahead and praise your way out" or "The joy of the Lord is your strength!" Then I looked around, and everybody had caught ahold of the praise, including the ushers whose fans were now flying in the air. Pretty soon I, along with the other young people, danced and praised God too. And although I didn't fully understand it all, something down inside of me knew that these old saints were receiving strength to make it through their night season.

When they praised the Lord, they seemed to be relaying heavenly messages from the throne of God to one another through the words of these songs. And right there, in the midst of their individual night seasons, the joy of the Lord seemed to fortify them on their journey. These joyful old saints commanded their souls to bless the Lord.

Knowing that the Lord was with them regardless of the season, these old saints praised the Lord in spite of their circumstances. These old saints knew that in His own perfect timing He would accomplish His purpose. These old saints had faith in God to bring them out of the dark season into the marvelous light of a new season, prepared and ready to go forth in their God-assigned purposes.

What My Old Grandmother Knew

After church on the ride home I would be so full of questions for my grandmother. She would always try her best to answer them in a way I could understand. I asked about the song "We'll Understand It Better By and By."

"Grandmother, Where is by and by? What is by and by?"

My grandmother, in her brilliant simplicity, would say, "Baby, just keep on living, and you will understand some things better when the time is right and your understanding grows."

That's the time when you will understand why things happen the way they do and the good that can come from it without being angry with God or holding grudges with other people because of it.

This meant to me that there were some things that I would experience in my life that I wouldn't readily understand the "why" until I was mature enough to know that God allows certain situation into my life for my making, which would help me understand the true meaning of this time frame called by and by; I pondered this for a long time.

When I asked my grandmother about the song "Trouble Don't Last Always," her answer was: "Baby, God is good and merciful, and just like the winter [which used to be terrible with all the snow and ice on the hills of Kansas City], troubled times won't last all year round. It's just for a season and then spring, summer, and fall weather will come again. Don't rush it, because to every season there is a purpose, and we need the winter season because the cold weather kills the germs and prepares the ground and the atmosphere for the spring growing season."

Then she would go on talking about the importance of every season, which meant to me that although some seasons may be very hard to endure, those seasons have a purpose in our lives, and they will only last for a while until they accomplish their purpose.

Well, sure enough just what my grandmother said about the winter season happened. The snow stopped falling, the sun reappeared, and the ice melted and turned to clear running water that softened the ground preparing it to receive seed for a new growing season. The trees budded with new life, the green grass spouted, and the birds sang their beautiful songs. We put away the winter coats and soon paraded around in our Easter spring frocks. Then summer came, and we pulled out our shorts and tops to enjoy the blessings of a new season.

I learned that just as the cold hard winter plays an important role in preparing the ground to ensure a "great harvest of crops" in the reaping season, so it is with those night seasons of preparation that will come in our lives.

God uses the night season as a time of growth and development in preparation for the "great harvest of souls" that He will produce through our lives in the reaping season as well.

The song "Something Inside Me Is Telling Me to Go Ahead" seemed to be the real encourager for the old saints because during this song they would march around the church with Holy Ghost laughter. They encouraged one another as they sang.

These old saints had an unseen helper, which was the Spirit of the living God abiding down inside of them. The Holy Spirit urged them to go forward through their difficult times and seasons.

Imagine that. It was as though they had a cheerleader, the Holy Ghost, down inside of them and a pep squad of praising believers surrounding, supporting, and rallying them to keep moving onward until they could make it through the night season to the glorious dawning of a new season.

After This

You Can't Park Here

That song reminded me of a book I once read titled: *You Can't Park Here*. The book basically reminded the reader that although we go through seasons of trials and tribulation in our lives, we're not to park in the midst of the situation and give up; but we have to keep moving and learning what God is teaching us through the tests and trials. So now whenever I am going through my darkest hours and discouragement urges me to park in my misery, I remember those old saints as they swayed, sang, and cheered each other on, with the words of that old song "Something Inside Me Is Telling Me to Go Ahead."

I now understand to a greater extent what the old saints knew and even why the old slaves who were on their journey to freedom adopted the practice of singing old inspirational hymns to get them through the night seasons. Those old songs not only contained words of encouragement that gave them the kind of joy that strengthened and helped them to endure their pain and suffering, but these old songs contained words that gave them godly directions that helped lead them to the promised land of a new season.

Those songs of praise have been passed on from generation to generation as a light of hope and guidance, and as a praise weapon of protection for all who are passing from one season to another, reminding us not to park in the midst of the pain of a particular season. Those old saints knew that when they sang those old songs, the "gates of hell could not prevail against them."

Like the old saints, we need to understand the significance of praising God at all times, regardless of the season. The old saints believed that when praises go up, God's blessings come down! We too must continue to praise God and share our faith and testimonies of victory with others, even in midst of the test.

We can let others know that whatever test and trial they're experiencing, God will never leave them or forsake them. And *after this*, God will most certainly bring them out of the darkness of their night seasons into the marvelous light of a new season, equipped and ready to fulfill their next kingdom assignment.

Chapter Four

My Personal Night Season

And we know that all things work together for good to those who love God, to those who are the called according to His purpose.
—*Romans 8:28, NKJV*

As I stated at the beginning of this book, I've been through many difficult night seasons in my life, as God continues to anoint, strengthen, and prepare me for the ministry assignments. However, there is one season that seemed more difficult than them all, and by the grace of God I want to share this particular personal night season with you in hopes that you will find strength, hope, and encouragement in the test and trial you are going through and to let you know that there is life after this.

I really don't know exactly when the season began because it all seemed so sudden. I just know that it seemed to incorporate a lifetime of everything I had ever learned in my walk with God and required every ounce of faith I could muster to help me make it through one of the darkest seasons of my life. The season included the terminal illness, loving supportive care, and death of my beloved husband of nearly forty years.

Noticing the Change

I started to notice significant changes in my husband's behavior and body that prompted me to ask, "Why is he so irritable? Why is everything so urgent with him all of a sudden? Why is he losing all that weight? Why is he so tired, and why is he not eating like he normally does?" I asked him, "Honey, have you been to see your doctor lately? I'll be glad to go with you if you'd like."

My husband's answer to everything was, "I am doing just fine." Of course I knew he wasn't as he lay around the house and slept more and more. His health was rapidly declining.

Finally, after much urging, and no signs of improvement, he felt so bad that he went to the emergency room to get checked out. Generally, during an emergency room visit you go through a few brief tests, some quick pokes, prodding, and a fleeting consultation concerning your results. The doctor gives you a prescription with a recommendation to see your regular physician for a follow-up, and out the door you go.

However, something about this visit was a lot more detailed. After hours of blood tests, x-rays, different doctors coming and going, the emergency room visit turned into a hospital admission and hours of waiting. Finally, the attending physician returned with much concern in his voice and spoke four words that would impact our lives forever.

My Personal Night Season

The Diagnosis

The doctor pronounced the findings: "It's stage IV cancer." Those words echoed like being inside a big hollow room. "What does that mean?" I asked. The doctor was about to simply turn and walk away after dropping an atomic bomb in our lives.

"He needs to see an oncologist, and your husband will need to do immediate chemotherapy and radiation and even then, his prognosis does not look good."

Thank God for the strength he gave my husband at that very moment. He seemed relieved to finally know what was wrong, but my heart sank, and my mind was racing all over the place. *Cancer*—the dreaded six-letter word no one wants to hear, not even with all of the latest medications, modern technology and living testimonies. My husband remained in the hospital for five weeks of intensive treatment, and the long night's journey began.

I wondered: "What am I going to do? How do I tell my children and grandchildren about the diagnosis, and how will they react to the news? How and when do I tell our family and close friends, with respect to the fact that my husband is such a private person?" The words of a song kept ringing in my heart, "If I ever needed the Lord before, I sure do need Him now!" I had to walk by faith and not by sight, believing that God was going to heal him because what would I do without my husband in my life?

> **If I ever needed the Lord before, I sure do need Him now!**

After This

My Reality Moment

As I drove home from the hospital after a very long day of being stunned by the critical news of my husband's illness, forty years of memories flooded my mind. After all, this wasn't just anybody lying in the hospital with the doctor's prognosis of possible death. This was my closest friend, my confidant, my first true love, the husband of my youth, the father of my children, the Paw Paw to our grandchildren, my earthly protector, my provider, and the person I expected to always be there for me and my family through old age. Not to mention, he was only sixty years old and too young to die.

Maybe if I tried shaking myself, I'd wake up from this awful nightmare, and it would all go away. You know, like those awful dreams we sometimes have that seem so real that you can feel and remember every awful detail. And when you finally wake up and realize it was only a bad dream you just start praising God and thanking Him that it was "only a dream" and the nightmare is over.

But the reality was, this was not a bad dream. I was wide awake and fully coherent and actually hearing the diagnosis. From extensive testing, a cancer specialist and several other doctors concluded that my husband indeed had stage IV cancer. They recommended radical radiation and chemotherapy. Immediately. I am so grateful for the kind of health insurance we had that covered everything, which was God showing me from the onset that He was with me.

However, despite my faith in God as a mighty healer, my reality was that my husband was now laying in a hospital bed with this cancer spread throughout his body, and there was nothing I could do about it but to pray and continue to trust God's plan and timing. While desperately trying to embrace the process, I tried to understand *why*.

Wow! Is this how Job felt when he received the news about his family crisis? Job fell to his knees. He struggled to gather his faith and positive thoughts. Job faithfully declared: "The LORD gives, and the LORD takes away. Blessed be the name of the LORD" (Job 1:21, CSB). As for me, all I could do was sing Smokie Norful's song "I Need You Now."

There's a real blessing in singing praises to the Lord in your hour of need. It is my weapon of praise.

I sat in my driveway for hours singing, praying, and looking at my husband's empty car in his usual space next to mine. I wondered if he'd ever pull in beside me again. It's crazy what you think about during a crisis moment. I looked at the grass that my husband always cut and whispered the craziest prayer to the Lord: "God, I know you're going to raise him up from this sickness. Who else will mow the lawn and trim the hedges and cut the back hill? Lord, you know that nobody else can manicure the yard quite like Larry. Amen." I know that God has a sense of humor and compassionately understands our crazy moments.

Lord, What About Our Family Plans?

We married when I was only nineteen, and he was only twenty-one years old. I left my father and mother's house and went directly to our house. I became one with him and cleaved to him only, as the Bible instructed us to do, never knowing what it was like to live alone. We grew through everything together. Regardless of our life situation, challenges, marital victories and disappointments, my husband would always love me, and I would always love him, and we would always be there for each other. The plan was to have two children, a boy and a girl, and God blessed us with two beautiful children, a girl who looked just like me and a boy who looked just like him. We have six beautiful grandchildren, who called us Maw Maw and Paw Paw. We were a family with a lot of family plans ahead of us.

With our children all grown up and out on their own, we were empty nesters with time to grow together in this season of our lives. We were growing older with all of the physical changes while learning to understand what beauty looks like at any age, getting our AARP cards, while keeping our vows made before God and a host of witnesses to stay together for better or worse, richer or poorer, in sickness and in health, until death would depart us—nearly forty years of going through it all.

We had plans to focus on God's will and each other, plans for retirement, plans to buy a retirement home (maintenance free), plans to further spoil those grandchildren while teaching them the ways of the Lord, and plans to leave them an inheritance. However, there was nothing in the plan for separation, not even by death, though we knew that death was inevitable for all human beings. There was no plan for either of us living all alone, eating alone, sleeping alone, retiring alone, or being alone.

No Longer the Counselor but the Counselee

At the time of my husband's illness, I was teaching my Crisis Counseling Class at Faith Bible College in Independence, Missouri, where I have taught crisis counseling and management for many years. I have taught countless numbers of student counselors what to expect, what to do, and where the source of your strength is in the midst of a major crisis situation. So with all the crisis training and the counsel that I had given to others, as well as the many personal crises I'd endured, surely I'd be able to navigate through the familiar crisis-management steps and make it through this major crisis with the help of the Lord.

As the counselee (the person in the midst of the crisis) everything I thought I knew suddenly became a giant blur. The steps I had taught others somehow seemed very difficult for me to remember, and no matter how supportive my family and extensive support team seemed to be, I still felt so isolated and all alone. Being the second of nineteen children, I always considered myself the big sister who could handle most anything with the help of the Lord, but not this time.

During this particular crisis I quickly realized that I was no longer the counselor, but I was the counselee in need of guidance. Thank God for the student counselors that I was teaching at the time in December 2011. My students (many of whom were ministers) became my counselors. They used everything they'd learned from crisis counseling and other classes to help me. They reminded me of the "Crisis Cycle of Emotions" and did an excellent job as counselors in every stage of my journey. I also had my personal family, church family, and friends as my support team.

Understanding the Crisis Cycle of Emotions

As I write about this Crisis Cycle of Emotions from the natural aspect of my own human emotions, it may seem somewhat strange to those who feel like super-human beings. However, we must remember that we were all created with real human emotions and a real need for God strength as we navigate through the different seasons of our lives, while being prepared by God for our kingdom assignments here on earth.

In crisis counseling we teach that there are four major stages that one can experience when walking through a crisis cycle, as experienced by Job and many others in the Bible. I created the acronym I-WAR to help my students remember the internal struggle one encounters during a crisis and quickly identify each stage of the crisis cycle. This also helps the counselor to immediately identify what stage of the crisis a counselee is currently going through, what the counselors should be doing, and the time frame it usually takes to appropriately navigate safely through the particular stage.

For your information I will briefly share the four stages of the crisis cycle. Please remember that the time it takes to move through the various stages can differ for each individual depending on their level of coping ability, faith in God and their support system.

The Four Stages of a Crisis Cycle (I-WAR)

I = Impact: The initial stage in which you are impacted by the news of the crisis and the stage in which all kinds of human emotions begin to flood your being. It is during this stage that you can be completely thrown out of balance physically, emotionally, and spiritually, and you need someone strong enough to support you where you are.
Usual time frame: several hours/days

My Personal Night Season

W = Withdrawal and Confusion: The stage in which you realize that the crisis is real and all the confusing details of your crisis situation start to resonate in your mind, with thoughts of wanting to be left alone. At this stage you cannot figure it out or get through it alone without God or a support system. Therefore, you must seek and receive constructive counsel to help move you along.
Usual time frame: several days/weeks

Note: Remember that during this stage of the crisis Satan loves to isolate hurting people so he can speak to your fragile heart and manipulate your mind, so you need to seek professional counsel/help as quickly as possible.

A = Adjustment: The stage in which you begin to adjust to the reality of your situation, and you begin to actively seek God's help along with other resources and progressive solutions to help move you through this critical night season toward your new season of hope, healing, and restoration.
Usual time frame: several weeks/months

R = Reconstruction and Reconciliation: The stage in which you have gotten through the pain and immobility of the crisis, and you are ready to rebuild trust and move forward in reconstructing your life and have found inner peace and reconciliation with others, understanding the process allowed by God. At this stage, forgiveness and healing are evident as you are ready to move confidently into your new season knowing that God will use all that you've been through and learned from the critical night season for your good and will use you to teach others how to navigate through their difficult night seasons.
Usual time frame: several months/years

Lord, I Need Your Help

At the time, I was somewhere between the I and the W (Impact, Withdrawal and Confusion). I was begging God to work a miracle of healing in my husband's body and raise him up, so we could tell the story of God's miraculous healing power. "Come on, Jesus, I've seen You do it so many times before, and I know You can do it again" was my continual prayer. I drew strength from my faith in the Lord Jesus Christ and hope from my family and other believers who were hoping against hope that he would pull through and make it.

I clung to God for help, as my emotions raced all over the place. I soon realized that even with the help of my support team, there were portions of this journey that I would be required to walk alone with God. And even knowing that God was with me, I still felt so alone, groping in the darkness of this unfamiliar territory. I found myself constantly repeating the following scripture:

> *Yea, though I walk through the valley of the shadow of death, I will fear no evil: for thou art with me; thy rod and thy staff they comfort me.*
> *Psalm 23:4, KJV*

> "Come on, Jesus, I've seen You do it so many times before, and I know You can do it again..."

Precious Revelation—It's Not All About Me

One evening, during one of my many stays with my husband at the hospital, God allowed me to look deeply into my husband's eyes and see and feel what he was feeling. I suddenly realized that the pain of what

My Personal Night Season

I was feeling during this season was nothing compared to the emotional and physical pain of what he was enduring. I could plainly see that my husband had accepted from the Lord that his time in this present life was nearing the end (even though I was not ready to accept it) and there was a peace there between him and God concerning this. However, in the midst of his peace and acceptance of death, I could also see the emotional worry of my husband, wondering what was going to happen to me, who would be left in the home alone, our children, and grandchildren.

My husband was always a great provider and protector for our family, rarely asking anyone but God for help in this area. He always assumed his position and responsibility as the head provider of his family. Not wanting to upset or worry me, he never discussed his concern, but I knew it was there. I knew I had to somehow let him know, without falling apart, that God was preparing me and that God was going to take care of me and the family so he could rest his mind. I could plainly hear the following scripture:

> *We then that are strong ought to bear the infirmities of the weak, and not to please ourselves.*
> *Romans 15:1, KJV*

From that point on I stopped focusing so much on my feelings and emotions and started focusing more on how he felt, and that's when the conversation with my husband changed. We began to talk the same language about eternal healing that comes from God and the joy of walking with God on another level. I let my husband know, in so many words, that regardless of what God decided concerning his healing, God was going to continue to be our family's great provider.

Oh, the peace that flooded my husband's being just knowing that I was prayerfully embracing God's process and provision for our lives and trusting God's sovereign decision, whatever the outcome. I too experienced the peace spoken of in Philippians 4:7, which kept my heart and mind in balance, through the help of my Lord and Savior Jesus Christ.

This God peace helped me to refocus my self-centered thoughts and worries so that I could better understand what my husband was going through, which also allowed me to clearly hear God in the process. It's simple human nature to sometimes focus on your own internal pain, anticipated loss, and future state of affairs during these difficult times. However, you must also realize the internal pain and the eternal feeling of separation that the person who may be about to leave this world and pass through the portal of death alone (unable to take their family with them) must be feeling and understand they need the greater support.

This godly support is not only needed for those who may be facing death, but for anyone who is facing a personal crisis, which generally involves some type of major loss or change, altering the course of one's life. I realized it was my time to bear the infirmity of my husband's illness, as his body was becoming weaker as a result of being ravished by the radiation and chemotherapy and also his concern for our family, should God choose the way of death as his eternal healing.

For those walking this similar path of testing and trials, please take a moment to do as I had to do as God revealed to me His eternal plan for my husband. Prayerfully step out of your own personal emotions and look at those facing the greatest challenge of their lives. Allow the strength you see in them (in the midst of their personal pain) to strengthen you. Forget about your own personal pain or fleshly desire so that you can unselfishly love and support them past their fear as they confidently trust in the Savior to safely guide them through the momentary portal of death, or any other life-changing circumstance, into the glorious awakening of their new season.

This is what Jesus wanted of His disciples when He asked them to pray and support Him past the fear of death to the secure and peaceful mind-set of "nevertheless not my will, but thine, be done" (Luke 22:42, KJV). After which, God dispatched angelic help from the heavenly sanctuary to strengthen Him and carry Him through.

And he was withdrawn from them about a stone's cast, and kneeled down, and prayed, Saying, Father, if thou be willing, remove this cup from me: nevertheless not my will, but thine, be done. And there appeared an angel unto him from heaven, strengthening him.
Luke 22:41–43, KJV

We must remember that just as Father God did for Jesus at the critical point of His journey, He will dispatch His angels to strengthen and help us as we are going through the most critical point in our night seasons.

The Treatment Is Not Working

Although I saw the peace of God grow stronger and stronger in my husband's spirit, I couldn't deny the fact that his physical condition was growing weaker.

The doctor delivered the news, "The treatment is not working, and it's best to stop." They suggested that I place him in a skilled nursing facility or take him home and utilize the service of hospice. All I could think of was the poem, "Footprints in the Sand." At this point I knew that there was only one set of footprints in the sand, and they belonged to my Lord and Savior Jesus Christ. He was carrying not only my dear husband, but He was carrying me too. I rested in knowing that His strength is perfect when our strength is gone.

I Want to Go Home

"I want to go home." My husband had had enough of the procedures, poking, and prodding.

Five weeks had passed since the diagnosis and treatments began, and we were now going home with hospice care. *Hospice* was a word I had always associated with death and never wanted to deal with. However, I never knew the blessings that these ministering angels actually bestowed upon the entire family during these times of crisis. This team of angels sent from God to strengthen me and my family via the Cross Roads Hospice Center of Kansas City was nothing but a blessing, as they helped my husband and each of us as we walked through the final days of my husband's life.

Then after being home for seven days (God's number of completion) and sharing some very intimate moments of family love and remembrances, early in the morning, on December 4, 2011 (my fifty-ninth birthday), God called my husband to his eternal home.

Numb, but Eternally Blessed

The days ahead were very difficult as we endured the funeral planning, the services, the burial, and the finality of my husband's departure. The truth is a part of me departed with him that day, the part that belonged exclusively to "us" being one flesh in marriage. That departure left a tear in my heart that only God and time could heal. Since I had no frame of reference for losing a father (because my father was still alive and well), I prayed earnestly for divine grace, mercy, and healing for my children and grandchildren. They would now have to lean solely on their heavenly Father to provide them comfort as well as fatherly wisdom, as they healed from the death of their father. I also prayed for my own strength knowing that I was now their only surviving parent.

Learning from the Process

When we face sickness, death, or the loss of anything that significantly changes our lives, there's a lot we can learn in this season of preparation. I learned from this process that there were negative things hindering growth in my life. I surrendered my will and allowed God to hammer, chisel, and prune those things from my life. And He strengthened the good things that were vital for my next kingdom assignment.

Remember the fruit of Spirit I talked about earlier? Well, I now realize that some of mine were beginning to wither on the vine while others lay dormant just ripe enough to be picked off by the enemy. I mean that if they weren't going to be used for God, then Satan was standing by ready to pick my fruit right off the vine for his own use. What a tragic thought! What valuable lessons I learned and precious words of revelation I received from the Lord during that season.

I know that the Lord did not take my husband because of any of my shortcomings or the need to strengthen me, but because the time of my husband's earthly assignment had ended. However, God did lovingly and strategically use the circumstances of his departure to test, prove, teach, strengthen, and prepare me tremendously for my next kingdom assignment, which included writing this book.

There Is Life After Death

There are many who've gone through a similar season, and you need to hear from someone who made it through a night season of death to let you know that there's life after death. I am a living witness that God was faithful in every area of my life during this season. He not only helped me to endure my process of development through many tests and trials, but He was also faithful in unfolding His master plan for my next kingdom assignment.

I know the Lord has a master plan for your life as well, and He will use the circumstances of your life to obtain the goal, if you trust His plan. It has been seven years since the death of my husband, and I've learned that not only is there life after death, but that life is meant to be an abundant life. I knew if I was ever to reach the place of abundance, I couldn't camp out at the place of grief and pain too long. Although grief and mourning has its place during a time of loss (for some a bit longer than others), it can easily become Satan's breeding ground for stagnation and spiritual death if you dig in and camp there too long.

It's my hope that the words of this book will give you a greater understanding of the process and help you make it through your night season with the joy of knowing that God loves you, God is with you, and He has a master plan for you.

Again, I remind you of what the old saints knew and the song that kept me through it all: Trouble Don't Last Always.

How grateful I am that even in the midst of my storm, God gave me hope. I am glad that the extent of my husband's

My Personal Night Season

illness didn't last too long. The Lord gave my husband peace and eternal joy that was undeniable. His last day on earth was filled with unspeakable joy and the soulful sound of the Victory Temple Christian Life Center's praise team, along with family and friends who came to his bedside and sang a medley of praise and worship songs that helped to usher him through the dark portal of death into the loving arms of Jesus. He was ushered to a place where God wipes away all tears and there is no more death, sickness, pain, or perils of living in this present world. What a blessing! The Book of Revelation puts it like this:

> *He will wipe away every tear from their eyes, and death shall be no more, neither shall there be mourning, nor crying, nor pain anymore, for the former things have passed away.*
> *Revelation 21:4, ESV*

God's Timing Is Always Perfect

Even when we don't understand, God's timing is always perfect. I am grateful for God's amazing grace in times like these. I cannot say that during my night season that I always understood the entirety of God's plan for my life. But I can affirm that God never left me. I was always learning as I groped in the darkness of my night season being equipped by God to fulfill my God-ordained purpose. And now after a period of healing and restoration, the blessings of what I learned through this trial have strengthen and prepared me for my new season. I've had the opportunity to walk with many widows and

> "Even when we don't understand, God's timing is always perfect."

grieving individuals in their season of pain. I've helped them understand that even in death God is good and has a great plan for their lives, letting them know that there is life after death and in fact it's meant to be an abundant life. And though they may not fully understand what is happening now, I tell them, "You will understand it better, by and by."

One of the questions that I really needed God to answer was, "Why did my husband have to die on my birthday?" I assumed I would never understand this, and I would never enjoy another birthday after this. Strangely on the day my husband died, I received a call from one of my cousins, a minister in Texas, extending her condolences and wishing me a happy birthday all in the same call. As I fought back the tears and a bit of discouragement, she went on to say, "God gave you a special birthday gift of Larry passing on your birthday."

"WHAT!" She must be tripping!!! I literally almost hung that phone up in pain, but the Spirit of the Lord calmed my spirit and whispered, "Listen."

She continued by letting me know that I may not understand it now, but I would understand it better by and by. There were those words again, words my grandmother and the old saints sang about.

Well, as the weeks and months passed away, my healing began, and before I knew it the first anniversary of my husband's death and my sixtieth birthday was knocking at my calendar door.

It should be noted that my children and family have always celebrated my birthday in royal style, but I wasn't looking forward to this birthday or the anniversary of my beloved husband's departure. One of my wishes for my sixtieth birthday was to be surrounded by my family and friends for my birthday celebration, so I requested a weekend slumber

My Personal Night Season

party leading up to the big day. I invited my nine sisters and ten of my best friends from over the years to spend the night in my new home—a parting blessing from my husband who God had blessed to make a great financial plan for me to be able to purchase a retirement home without having to take out a mortgage. What a blessing!

As everyone gathered the night before my birthday in all their crazy pajamas, with good food, gifts, and funny stories about my life, somehow the evening turned into a joyous prelude leading up to the big sixtieth birthday celebration and the anniversary of my husband's departure. My birthday was filled with laughter, love, festivities, and blessings, and I soon realized that there was really no space for sadness concerning my husband's death. As I lovingly thought about Larry throughout the day, it was only thoughts of love and happiness and of him smiling down upon me, because I was celebrating life and not death.

Just think, if my husband would have died the day before my birthday, I probably would've cried and been so depressed when my birthday came that I wouldn't have enjoyed my actual birthday. Or if he would've died the day after my birthday, the anxiety of knowing the anniversary day was coming would have been so overwhelming that I wouldn't have been focused enough to enjoy my actual birthday. So God gave me the "special gift" of Larry passing on my birthday. He wanted me to always celebrate another year of life, good memories, family, and friends. Each year my birthday continues to be a wonderful celebration of life. I actually felt my husband smiling, with his big beautiful boyish grin, letting me know that this is how he wanted me to continue each year, with no sad day of remembrance concerning his departure.

Now in this season of by and by, I have a clearer understanding of exactly what my cousin meant and why God allowed it to happen the way it did. What an awesome God we serve!

Out With The Old

There were so many days right after my husband's death that I didn't know how I was going to emotionally make it through. The reality that my husband lived in heaven, and I was still here on earth, living alone in the house we'd shared for over thirty years was overwhelming. The lingering smells of his cologne, the afterglow of his presence, and so many memories were everywhere. I pulled into my driveway so many nights and just parked for hours and wept. I didn't want to go in the house and be alone. The twenty-four-hour Walmart became a solace for me just because it was all lit up, and people were shopping like it was broad daylight. Who does that? I guess me and anyone who's learning how to keep it moving during the night season of testing and preparation by any means necessary.

After many months of struggling to get through my grief and finally feeling the strong healing hand of the Lord upon my life, I knew I could no longer park here (the point of my grief and suffering). I felt the gentle prodding from the Lord telling me to move on, and I knew that it would be in my moving forward that God was going to clearly speak to me about His master plan for my life.

Having something productive to do—like renovating my new house—during this season was a real medicine for me. The precious time spent alone with God, painting, hammering, and singing praises to Him allowed me the time to focus on my next kingdom assignment without the worries of a monthly mortgage. This old house that I was working on was

My Personal Night Season

a metaphor of what God was doing in my life. When I purchased this beautiful, all brick, custom ranch, it was gorgeous with such good bones, but it was so stuck in the past with seventies décor; it needed a twenty-first-century renovation. I beamed as the contractors knocked down walls, making it an open concept that allowed the light to come through, adding much more space for entertaining family and friends. Rooms that had never been used were being brought to life with new paint, lighting, flooring, furnishing, and wall décor. Sometimes it pays to watch HGTV for ideas on how to bring an old house back to life again. All of the old useless stuff was thrown in the dumpster as the sound of the big delivery truck brought in the new materials, and the transformation was miraculous.

Spiritually, that's just what God is doing with each of us as He takes us through seasons of transformation. He's knocking down internal walls that have not only separated us from people and blocked our purpose, but also have prevented the light of His glory from shining through our lives. As the master builder, He's not trying to destroy the house He created, but instead He's transforming it and shouting, "Out with the old and in with the new!"

I'm not saying that God is telling you to physically move from your home as I was led to do, but He is most certainly telling you it's time for a spiritual move, as you go through your night season of preparation. And when the season of preparation is over, you must not linger there, but learn from the lessons you've endured and keep moving mentally, physically, and spiritually. God has a reward awaiting you, along with instructions for your next kingdom assignment.

My friend, if you have gotten spiritually or physically stuck, please take your life out of park and remember that you can't park here. You are just passing through this season

After This

of preparation, and trust me, it won't last always. It's a new season in my life, and I don't want to be stumbling around where God was in the past, trying to hold onto yesterday. But I am determined to be where God is this very day, equipped and ready to launch into my next kingdom assignment, where abundant life awaits me *after this*.

Chapter Five

He Restoreth My Soul

...He leadeth me beside the still waters. He restoreth my soul.
—*Psalm 23:2–3a, KJV*

One of the most memorable messages that I've heard my pastor preach was titled "If You Can Rest, You Can Recover."

Never let anyone tell you that rest and restoration are not important during and after a night season of testing and preparation. After any major surgery, illness, or crisis, the doctor may prescribe medication or even moderate exercise, but one of the most important things prescribed for proper healing and recovery is rest.

When boxers are fighting, at an appointed time, the referee rings the bell, signaling to each of the fighters that it's time to stop fighting and go to their individual corners to rest and recover. During this rest and recover time, the coach pours water on the fighter's head and applies salve to any wounds sustained. And they speak encouraging words to the fighter's spirit and give strategic instructions to equip them for a win against their opponent.

During the night season of test and trials there's nothing like hearing the Shepherd's comforting voice and receiving His guidance. Sometimes this encouragement will come from the comforting voice of an earthly shepherd (leader), who recognizes the struggle and can speak comfort and peace. There's such peace that comes from knowing that the Great Shepherd is present in our corner to provide what we need during the battle. Hear what the psalmist says:

> "There's such peace that comes from knowing that the Great Shepherd is present in our corner..."

The LORD is my shepherd; I shall not want. He maketh me to lie down in green pastures: he leadeth me beside the still waters. He restoreth my soul.
Psalm 23:1–3a, KJV

So often as human beings we don't realize when we've reached our limit. Therefore, we push past our human capability, or we allow others to push us past our human limitation causing us to experience the danger of burnout.

Sheep are vulnerable to wolves and other predators, therefore, they need the guidance of the shepherd to gently prod them and make sure they are safe, nourished, and cared for all the days of their life. We people of God are the sheep of God's pasture (Psalm 100:3), and much like sheep, we have limitations. The Lord, our Good Shepherd, knows just how much we can bear and when it's time to nudge us and make us rest.

He Restoreth My Soul

Pastors and organizational leaders, please be aware that the enemy wants to destroy you most of all, because he knows if he can kill the head, the tail will be easy prey. You must recognize when it's time for you to slip away from the battle or your everyday grind for a time of rest in the presence of the Lord, along with times of relaxation and family leisure. There have been seasons in my life when I pushed past my limit, and a friend invited me to stay in a plush, comfortable, and quiet place for a season of rest and relaxation, but I was too busy. As a result I became so weary that I began to operate in the flesh. Sound familiar? There is such a danger in trying to do kingdom work when you are worn and stressed out. During these times the fruit of the Spirit is not properly operating in your life, and the flesh will get loose. The flesh (human emotions and behaviors) can get loose in many ways, but mainly through your tired body and stressed-out mind. This can cause you to display no patience, no goodness, no kindness, no meekness, loose lips, and you know the rest of your fleshly behaviors.

Jesus Always Knew When It Was Time for Him and the Apostles to Rest

And the apostles gathered themselves together unto Jesus, and told him all things, both what they had done, and what they had taught. And he said unto them, Come ye yourselves apart into a desert place, and rest a while: for there were many coming and going, and they had no leisure so much as to eat. And they departed into a desert place by ship privately.

Mark 6:30–32, KJV

Sometimes the needs of people can become so great that you forget to take care of you. The apostles had gotten so caught up in the work that they had no time for leisure or to even eat. That's too busy! Not only in doing the work of the ministry, but also when going through great tests and trials, you must be aware of your own human limits and listen for the Great Shepherd as He leads and instructs you to come away and rest. This rest and restoration is not just for physical strengthening and restoration, but also a time for spiritual restoration, a time to pray, to get in the Word, and hear from God.

> *And a great windstorm arose, and the waves beat into the boat, so that it was already filling. But He was in the stern, asleep on a pillow. And they awoke Him and said to Him, "Teacher, do You not care that we are perishing?"*
> Mark 4:37–38

Even in the midst of a storm, Jesus was found peacefully resting so He could be refreshed and ready to rebuke the raging storm.

People will also be looking for you and insisting you get back in the saddle to meet their needs. But remember, to effectively be prepared for ministry you must stop, rest, and be restored physically and spiritually so you can be equipped to face your next test or your next kingdom assignment.

Others May Not Understand Your Need to Slip Away

There will be times when others get upset because of your need to slip away and get into the presence of the Lord. You just have to do like Mary who separated herself from her sister Martha and the daily grind of service to others to sit at the feet of Jesus. Martha wanted Mary to stay in the kitchen and continue to serve. She commanded Jesus to make Mary go back in the kitchen and work! Notice how Jesus approves of Mary's decision to slip away to get in His presence:

> *And Jesus answered and said unto her, Martha, Martha, thou art careful and troubled about many things: But one thing is needful: and Mary hath chosen that good part, which shall not be taken away from her.*
> *Luke 10:41–42, KJV*

There are those who complain to God in prayer and to others (in their selfishness) concerning your need to take a break from the grind of daily ministry to be restored in the presence of the Lord. Be like Mary and ignore the vocal opposition and make your way to the feet of Jesus.

Note:
- You cannot continuously pour into the lives of others and never take time to be poured into (restored and refreshed).
- Never be so busy "doing the work of the Lord" that you forget about "the Lord of the work."

Chapter Six

An Avalanche in the Valley

My brethren, count it all joy when you fall into various trials.
—*James 1:2, NKJV*

While writing this book, I had a great avalanche hit my life. Webster defines an avalanche as a sudden arrival or occurrence of something in overwhelming quantities. Just as I was beginning to see the light at the end of this long journey, an overwhelming landslide happened in my life that would again test everything in me as I was being prepared for my next kingdom assignment.

Water-Walking Faith

First, God was requiring me to do something that would truly require absolute faith in Him as my Lord, Savior, and Provider. As a chosen vessel being tested and proven by God for each new level of ministry assignment, you will at times be asked to do some things you have never done before. It's easy to say that we have faith until the time comes when we must let go of the boat (our familiar comfort zone), and God bids us to come and walk on water (a naturally impossible feat). This means if we're going to truly let go, we will have to fully trust God, believing that He won't let us drown and that He knows how to safely navigate us to our prepared destinations.

> *Trust in the L*ORD *with all thine heart; and lean not unto thine own understanding. In all thy ways acknowledge him, and he shall direct thy paths.*
> *Proverbs 3:5–6, KJV*

Wow! That's a tall order to be asked not to lean to your own understanding. After all we are taught to think for ourselves and not to make foolish moves that could potentially harm us. We usually want to be the driving force in the step-by-step plans for our lives. But somehow, when you know that you know that it is God orchestrating a master plan for your life, there's a confident peace that accompanies your faith. If you can keep your eyes on Jesus (like Peter needed to do when he walked on water), you will see the Lord perform a miracle of faith for you, too, right there in the midst of your storm.

> *And Peter answered him and said, Lord, if it be thou, bid me come unto thee on the water. And he said, Come. And when Peter was come down out of the ship, he walked on the water, to go to Jesus.*
> *Matthew 14:28–29, KJV*

And now God was asking me to do something that for me seemed like an impossible request. After twenty-one years

An Avalanche in the Valley

of working on a job that I dearly loved and considered one of my greatest assignments in ministry as well as an essential source of my income, the Lord was asking me (without a plan of my own) to resign from my job and submit my two-week notice. The Lord had been orchestrating circumstances on my job for some time, preparing me for the day when I'd have to let go of the boat and allow Him to take full control of the wheel of my life. I just didn't think it would happen so suddenly.

The orchestration of how God used the circumstances on my job to help prepare me for the next level of ministry is a whole other book, so stay tuned.

Again remember, this test and lesson plan was specifically orchestrated by God for me. Your test will be totally different because the Lord knows what it takes for each of us to be tested and proven as vessels fit for His use in our individual kingdom assignments. In all that I had been through on my job, which at times was very difficult, there was always a confident peace

> "Again remember, this test and lesson plan was specifically orchestrated by God for me."

and blessed assurance that God was preparing me for something I would need to be available for and also strong and resilient enough to handle.

After leaving my job, still in some ways trying to lean to my own understanding, God allowed me a short period to rest (mentally and physically) to recover from what I had come through while on my job. Following a brief period of rest and recovery, I clearly heard the Lord say that my parents would be my next kingdom assignment. I know that much of our theology or doctrinal beliefs would have us to believe that our ministry is primarily in the church, but this next kingdom assignment was as important as any revival, educational seminar, classroom teaching, motivational-speaking engagement, community awareness challenge, mentoring at a training camp, or any of the other ministry assignments God has assigned me to do. This next ministry assignment would require a great deal of my spiritual, mental, and physical strength to be successful.

Strapping on My Boots

I come from a very large family, and we always talked of how blessed we were to have both our parents still alive and feisty as ever in their eighties. My mom, who was the stronger of the two healthwise, was always on the go, being faithful on the Mother's Board at church or with her community group of senior ladies, who was always up to something adventurous or most importantly orchestrating one of our many family gatherings. My dad, who was more confined due to his inability to walk, was still as lively, demanding, and hilarious as ever. We watched them navigate through the winter season of their lives with so much grace and love for our family.

As I considered my new kingdom assignment from the Lord, I was grateful that God had made a way for me to be off from work with the time and ability to consistently be with them and able to meet their mounting needs, along with the help of my other family members. They seemed to be adapting to their new physical status (driving me a little crazy competing for attention), but otherwise doing pretty well and loving the fact that I had more time to spend with them.

About two months into my new assignment, I noticed that my mom was having a lot of difficulty with her breathing, and after taking her to the doctor to check it out, her doctor diagnosed her with a chronic breathing condition and prescribed a breathing machine that seemed to help her breathe easier. But this confined her more and more to the house because of the machine's limitations. I watched as my mom's steps seemed to become slower, and she began to lose a lot of weight, despite what she ate. It really concerned me and made me have flashbacks concerning my husband's illness.

About the same time, I noticed that my dad's health began to decline, as he worried about my mom to the point of having to be hospitalized himself. For days my dad sat in the hospital refusing to eat or properly take his meds. Dad hated hospitals, and he wanted to go home. He was worried about my mom's welfare, and she worried about him.

As my mom worried and waited for my dad to recover in the hospital, I noticed that my mom's health condition began to take its toll on her mentally and physically. She worried about how she would be able to effectively help take care of my dad in her weakened condition, even after being assured that I, along with my siblings were going to take care of them. Finally, my mom's condition weakened to the point that she had to be hospitalized in an effort to stabilize her breathing and get her strong again. Now both of them were in the hospital at the same time.

The Walls Were Beginning to Crumble

Talk about an avalanche all at once! Now both of my parents were in the hospital in very poor condition. Because my mom had successfully been through this type of hospitalization before, we were pretty confident that the doctors would get her breathing back on track and send the release for her to go home in a few days. My dad, however, whose health was steadily declining, had us seriously worried whether or not he'd make it out alive. Such a roller coaster ride of emotions as I tried to exhibit a spirit of calmness and peace in the midst of this impending avalanche.

A Call for the Prayer Warriors

My family sent out a desperate cry throughout the body of Christ for prayer warriors to pray like never before for our parents' healing and recovery. Day and night we set up a huge family and friends camp in the hospital waiting room, covering my mother and father with much prayer and staying right there with them.

My dad, who was the sickest, seemed to be recovering nicely, but my mom didn't seem to be thriving or breathing any better. One evening I slipped to my mother's bedside and recognized that there seemed to be no fight left in her (keep in mind she was a real fighter). I talked to my mom about our entire family wanting her to get up from this bed of affliction and fight for her life like she always did and live.

Thy Will Be Done

One day my mom confidently beckoned me close to her bedside and let me know that she was praying, but her prayer was very different. My mother was praying for the family, praying that we would be strong and accept the will of God for her life. I immediately saw in my mother's eyes, what I had seen in my husband's eyes when I realized he had accepted the will of God for his life, and he knew it was his time to go. My mom shared with me that she was tired, and she knew her time to be with the Lord was fast approaching. I silently wept on the inside, because I knew I needed to try and be strong outwardly. God's amazing grace was upon me. My mother let me know that she had looked beyond her present sickness and that she had experienced an encounter with the Lord, speaking of it as a beautiful trip she was about to take free of all worries and pain. A trip she was ready to make.

This is the state of mind that I believe only those believers who are ready and know that they are about to transition to the promised life can fully understand and be so peaceful about. My mother had such a peaceful confident spirit as she took my hand and told me her desire for a joyous home-going celebration and the things she wanted added to her obituary—the one she had already written. She told me that she had signed a do not resuscitate order, knowing she would soon be going home to be with the Lord, and she did not want any of her children having to make the decision as to when.

To tell the truth, I really wanted to scream and fight for her, because I wasn't ready to lose my mother after having her for nearly sixty-four years of my life. My mother had such a calm resolve about herself as she began to minister to me with her eyes filled with tears. She told me that God was with her, and she knew it was her time to make her final earthly lap of this life's journey. It's amazing what you can endure when you know it is God's will, so I quietly whispered, "Thy will be done."

I went to the bathroom to gather myself, and after doing so I knew I needed to quickly tighten up my spiritual boots and become a soldier on assignment to prepare my family for the soon departure of our mother—an assignment I had to complete without frightening my family or shattering their hopes of her recovery.

After This

The Final Lap of the Journey

My dad would be the hardest, or so I thought. I, along with some of my siblings, went to finally share with him just how sick our mom really was and to prepare him to visit our mother for the last time while she was still alive. There seemed to be angels on assignment throughout Research Medical Center, because the staff began to move like soldiers, helping to make sure my dad could be safely transported to my mother's room in case of a medical breakdown. But my dad, who on this day was extremely alert, as though the angels were assisting him, was already fully prepared to take what he somehow knew would be his final lap of the journey with my mom here on earth.

He told me, "I dreamt of your mother the night before, and I want desperately to visit with her. I know her time is fast approaching, and I don't want anyone to hinder me or be afraid for me."

So without much assistance, my dad lifted himself into the wheelchair to begin what would be his final visit with my mom, the woman he deemed as his first love. My parents' love story has many chapters, some good times and some very difficult times, but what was always true is this, they always had a special love for each other. They were always destined to be together in this winter season of their lives.

As we wheeled my dad into my mom's room, there seemed to be a beautiful glow about my mother, and although she spoke no words because of being sedated, there was a sense that the two of them were communicating without words, something that only they could understand. With tears in his eyes, my dad asked, "Will everyone step out of the room and allow me time alone with your mother?" It was the time

I knew they needed to say goodbye on this side of life.

I noticed a change in my dad's demeanor after he talked with Mom. He exhibited a confident strength, as our father, somehow knowing that we would soon be without our mother, and he wanted us to know without specific words that we still had a father, and that he would help us make it through this.

Heavenly Wings from Heaven

Early the next morning, September 2, 2016, my mother received her heavenly wings and took her flight to glory, surrounded by her children, family, and friends. What a solemn but loving assembly on that day, as all of our family and friends and even the doctors and nurses joined us in tears and prayer as we saw our mother lying in such a perfect state of peace. We knew she was now eternally healed and safely in the arms of her loving Savior.

> *I noticed a change in my dad's demeanor after he talked with Mom.*

Another Set of Wings, Much Too Soon...

My dad was discharged from the hospital the day following my mother's earthly departure. Like a strong fatherly soldier, he marched with us through the funeral services and burial of our mother with the strength of an eagle. I watched, as my dad masked his pain to impart strength to each of us as we said our earthly goodbyes to our mother, somehow knowing he would see her again real soon.

After a few days of watching my father stare blankly in the distance, I knew that my kingdom assignment with both my parents would soon be coming to an end. My family tried desperately to cheer my dad up and stand in the gap for the emptiness he felt in the loss of our mother. I, along with my youngest brother, temporarily moved in with my dad to ensure he would never have to worry about being placed in a nursing home or feel alone after the passing of our mother. Each of my siblings set a rotating schedule for making sure my dad was well cared for, along with the loving care of the hospice angels, hoping the presence of family, especially all of his children, would cheer him back to life again.

But just fifty-seven days after the death of our mom, after making sure all was well with his soul and all his children, on October 29, 2016, my dad received his heavenly wings. He peacefully closed his eyes in death, surrounded by his children, joining my mother and all of his loved ones who had gone on before, now eternally healed and resting in the loving arms of Jesus.

What an avalanche of death this was for me and my family to lose both the matriarch (Mom) and the patriarch (Dad) all within a fifty-seven-day landslide. To say that we needed much prayer and time to grieve, rest, heal, and recover would be an understatement.

The Power of an Avalanche—Let It Work for Your Good

After the impact of losing both of our parents and going through the initial pain and healing process, I researched and learned some amazing facts about the positive power of an avalanche.

A study with the WSL-Institute for Snow and Avalanche Research SLF, Davos demonstrates that the destructiveness

An Avalanche in the Valley

of an avalanche also has positive aspects for nature. It creates environmental conditions, which enable an entire range of plant species to survive and even thrive due to the large cracks it leaves in its path. An avalanche enables much more light to hit the soil and provides a source for more water and nutrients to penetrate the otherwise hardened grounds making it more productive.

As a result of the avalanche of death that God allowed into my family's life, I have witnessed some positive effects:

- Some of my family members, whose hearts had been so hardened by the trials of life, have benefitted from the many tears (water) that flowed from this devastation, water that actually softened the ground of their hearts, allowing the nutrients of God's Word to penetrate their hearts and minds, allowing the light of His Son, Jesus Christ to shine through the cracks of their broken hearts to generate healing in many ways. (My mama prayed so hard that their hearts would someday be softened.)

- What we thought might happen as a result of the death of our parents has had the opposite effect on my family as a whole. Instead of division and confusion, we have in many ways banded closer together, knowing we are all we have. My mother and father always said, "At the end of the day, [besides God] all you really have is family," and the Morgan crew is such a unique family.

God has created such an environment of love and healing that we can clearly see the road ahead and discern that at the end of this devastating season, there will be a harvest of family love, forgiveness, growth, and unity. This devastating avalanche forced us to work together, which may never have occurred without these two precious seeds being planted in the ground, watered and nourished by our many tears. I now realize that the planting of these two seeds will someday produce a full harvest of blessings that will bless and bring salvation to many in our family and beyond. Hear what the scripture says about the planting of a seed:

> *Very truly I tell you, unless a kernel of wheat [seed] falls to the ground and dies [is planted], it remains only a single seed. But if it dies, [is planted] it produces many seeds [a harvest].*
>
> *John 12:24, NIV*

A harvest of blessings can be shared with others experiencing similar situations, teaching them that there is abundant life and a godly purpose, even after an avalanche such as this.

I know that God has a divine purpose in all of this, and it is "working together for my good" and for the good of my entire family who loves the Lord and are called according to His purpose. I know that we may not presently understand it all, but we will certainly understand it even better by and by.

But even now, I can feel God's hand at work in the transition of my parents. I blame God for nothing, because I know He has a master plan, which encompasses all of this. I know that my parents' works will follow them, and I am assured that the mantle that they left behind for God's glory will be picked up and carried on by those of us who are assigned to do even greater works than they did. I believe it is designed by God for each generation to carry on the good works of their ancestors and build on it to an even greater extent to accomplish all that God has planned.

An Avalanche in the Valley

I am grateful to have been blessed by God with two great people that I had the privilege to call my parents. And I am thankful that God gave me strength and the desire to fulfill this awesome part of my kingdom assignment. I know that someday when this life is over, I will see them again happy and carefree, somewhere around the throne of God.

Chapter Seven

God Has a Master Plan

*"For I know the plans I have for you," declares the L*ORD*, "plans to prosper you and not to harm you, plans to give you hope and a future."*

—*Jeremiah 29:11, NIV*

When we're going through our night season of testing and preparation, we may wonder, "Where is God? Is God aware of what I'm going through, and how will this situation end?" We may even wonder, "Is this some kind of punishment for the former sins I have committed against God?" But take heart, God has a master plan for your life. He has no desire for you to be destroyed, but rather His thoughts toward you are thoughts of peace and not evil, to give you an expected end. And although we may get off the intended path and may be suffering the consequences of our own sinful actions, God knows how to use the circumstances in our lives as part of His lesson plan to draw us back to the designated path again.

During your preparation season God may choose a lesson plan in which he allows Satan to test you because you're upright like Job. God may even choose to use the consequences of your own sinful choices as a part of your test plan, just as He did with King David, who willingly sinned with Bathsheba and had to learn some very difficult lessons in the classroom of life. Later David cried out to God in repentance, as he returned to God's path for his life (Psalm 51:1–10) and was used mightily by God. Whatever God's path of preparation, please be assured that He has a master plan for you.

> "Whatever God's path of preparation, please be assured that He has a master plan for you."

Surrendering to His Plan

One of the hardest things for us as human beings to do is to surrender our will to that of another. This is because it requires fully trusting someone else with your life, and although everybody cannot be trusted with your life, God your maker certainly can. To fully trust God's plan for your life, you must be willing to surrender your carnal will to His sovereign will. You must also have confident faith in His plan, His timing, and His method of achieving His master plan for you.

Chosen by God

The story of Joseph, which spans from Genesis 37–50, displays God's master plan for a young man whose journey would take him through many pitfalls, tests, and trials as God prepared him for his kingdom assignment. When Joseph was young, God revealed to him in a dream the call of God that was upon his life. Though Joseph did not fully understand all that the dream would come to mean, he certainly knew that he had been chosen by God, and he believed that God had a great plan for his life.

How excited this young fellow must have been as the dream revealed him to be the future leader of his family with great authority. Joseph was so excited and perhaps a wee bit prideful and boastful that he ran and told his dream to his older brothers, who were already jealous and hated him because of the favor shown to him by his father. Let's observe his brothers' and his father's reaction to Joseph's dream:

> *He said to them, "Listen to this dream I had: We were binding sheaves of grain out in the field when suddenly my sheaf rose and stood upright, while your sheaves gathered around mine and bowed down to it." His brothers said to him, "Do you intend to reign over us? Will you actually rule us?" And they hated him all the more because of his dream and what he had said. Then he had another dream, and he told it to his brothers. "Listen," he said, "I had another dream, and this time the sun and moon and eleven stars were bowing down to me." When he told his father as well as his brothers, his father rebuked him and said, "What is this dream you had? Will your mother and I and your brothers actually come and bow down to the ground before you?" His brothers were jealous of him, but his father kept the matter in mind.*
> *Genesis 37:6–11, NIV*

The reaction from Joseph's family is not uncommon. Sometimes even members of your own family cannot handle the scope of God's plan for your life, which when revealed before its time, can cause hatred, envy, and jealousy to take place, wreaking all kinds of devastating schemes to stop the plan God has for you. Therefore, there will be times in your life that your dreams and visions will have to remain hidden in God until the time of fulfillment is ready. This story reveals that the favor of God over your life will not always seem fair to those who do not understand the assignment or call over your life, nor the level of responsibility required of those who have been chosen by God for a specific weighty task. According to Joseph's dream, God's plan was to someday elevate Joseph to a position of leadership ruling with authority over his family.

Satan's Plan Is to Steal, Kill, and Destroy

Satan wants to stop the plan of God for your life. Therefore, the enemy will use anyone who will yield themselves as conduits to try to steal, kill, and destroy your God-ordained dreams, in hope of killing God's master plan for you. Joseph's brothers, like so many others, can be referred to as "haters" or "dream killers." These individuals see you as a threat or a hindrance to who they believe themselves to be. They will try to eliminate you or attempt to destroy your character by any means necessary with great ambitions to elevate themselves to a position of authority—positions that were never assigned to them, nor do they have the ability to handle. We must all realize that elevation (godly positioning) as well as the ability to handle the task come from God. Listen to the psalmist as he explains the source of promotion:

God Has a Master Plan

For promotion cometh neither from the east, nor from the west, nor from the south, but God is the judge: he putteth down one, and setteth up another.

Psalm 75:6–7, KJV

Let's see how Joseph's brothers sought to eliminate him:

"Here comes that dreamer!" they said to each other. "Come now, let's kill him and throw him into one of these cisterns and say that a ferocious animal devoured him. Then we'll see what comes of his dreams." When Reuben heard this, he tried to rescue him from their hands. "Let's not take his life," he said. "Don't shed any blood. Throw him into this cistern [dark hole] here in the wilderness, but don't lay a hand on him." Reuben said this to rescue him from them and take him back to his father. So when Joseph came to his brothers, they stripped him of his robe—the ornate robe he was wearing—and they took him and threw him into the cistern. The cistern was empty; there was no water in it.

Genesis 37:19–24, NIV

Here we can plainly see the plan of the enemy to strip Joseph of his royal robe, which represented the authority, favor, and blessing bestowed upon him by his father and a sign of his royal anointing. But remember, God always has a ram in the bush. When his brother Reuben heard the plan to kill Joseph, the wisdom and salvation of God was upon him as he sought to save Joseph's life. Reuben spoke to his brothers and said, "Let's not take his life," so they didn't kill him. Instead, intending to let him die there, they threw him into a pit (dark well) with no water.

After This

God's Vehicle to Transport Joseph

Remember at the beginning of the book I told you that God will use whatever vehicle He chooses to transport you to your appointed destiny. For Joseph, God sent a caravan of Ishmaelites (God's chosen vehicle for Joseph) loaded with precious spices and provisions to take him down to Egypt. Now listen, as God uses Judah to utter wisdom in the ears of his brothers:

> *What will we gain if we kill our brother and cover up his blood? Come, let's sell him to the Ishmaelites and not lay our hands on him; after all, he is our brother, our own flesh and blood.*
> Genesis 37:26–27, NIV

Sometimes the vehicle that God uses is not what we expected, but it's what will do the job and get us to our place of destiny. Joseph might've expected a royal carriage or maybe he expected his Daddy to ride in on a camel and save the day. But those vehicles couldn't take him to his destiny. God used the Midianite travelers and Ishmaelites to transport and set Joseph up for his kingdom assignment. God knew the right vehicle to get him to the right place.

What vehicle are you expecting to take you to your destiny? Don't be surprised if it's different than what you expected. Remember Moses? His vehicle to the palace was not a royal carriage, but started in a handmade basket floating up the Nile River, transporting him to the palace, his place of preparation. Or how about David? His vehicle to kingship started out in the field as a young shepherd boy tending and protecting his father's flock as God prepared him for the greater of work as a warrior who would someday protect and rule the kingdom.

We must trust the vehicle that God sends our way and believe that it's the best method to transport us to our assigned place of destiny. Be careful not to judge the vehicle by the way it looks, but see with eyes of faith a glorious vehicle (God's glory train) transporting you through your journey of preparation and ultimately to your kingdom assignment.

Character Building 101

In preparation for this next level kingdom assignment, we will be required to go through a season of Character Building 101. In reading the story of Joseph, we become increasingly aware of the fact that Joseph's character needed some tweaking and adjustment before he could be released by God to fully operate in his kingdom assignment. Let's look at one of the major character-building components necessary as we move to the next level.

- Humility: The higher God takes us, the more humble we have to be.

Joseph needed a lesson in humility before he could successfully fulfill the plan of God upon his life. We see Joseph's flesh on display as he parades around in his coat of many colors and the announcement of his dreams with much pride and arrogance of becoming the future leader over his household. Not to mention the favor and special attention shown to him by his father. How humbling for this favored son with his future dreams as a leader to be stripped and thrown into a dark muddy pit by those closest to him. Before we can truly go up, we must come down from any attitude of arrogance, pride, or self-glory. For Joseph the dark pit left him in low estate, dependent, and alone in the presence of God.

For those who are in the midst of their preparation season and experiencing a dark season of despair and loneliness, please remember that it is in the dark room that a picture is fully developed with clarity. Likewise, God is developing you in the dark room of adversity so that the distinct picture of your kingdom assignment can become crystal clear. Joseph had to be developed in every area of his life so that he, as well as others, could see with clarity God's master plan for his life. Again, these test and trials can certainly look as if the enemy has thrown you into a dark pit and God has forgotten you, but please be assured that God is still very much in control, and He has a master plan at work for you.

Joseph Is Rescued from the Pit

Joseph's assignment would not leave him to be destroyed in the dark pit, therefore, God rescued him from the pit so that he could proceed with his lesson plan designed to move him closer to his kingdom assignment.

> *Then as the Midianite [and Ishmaelite] traders were passing by, the brothers pulled Joseph up and lifted him out of the pit, and they sold him to the Ishmaelites for twenty shekels of silver. And so they took Joseph [as a captive] into Egypt.*
>
> Genesis 37:28, AMP

Remember in chapter 3 the section on "You Can't Park Here"? Joseph's story is an epic reminder that although things get dark and rough along the journey, you must continue to move through your test and trials as the Lord orders your steps moving you toward your destiny. Joseph could have parked in his disappointment and sorrow and had a pity

God Has a Master Plan

party in the pit, but he kept moving. He trusted God's plan for his life. Joseph moved in faith and boldly mounted his God-ordained vehicle with strangers (the Ishmaelites and the Midianites), who God used to transport him to his next classroom of learning, Egypt. Egypt was God's appointed destination for Joseph's school of preparation. Although Joseph went through many twist and turns on his journey to Egypt, God was with him every step of the way.

Just as with Joseph, God has a place custom-designed to equip you for the special assignment that is over your life. Whatever it takes, God knows how to navigate your life's situation to get you there. It is very important that you don't allow the pain of what you are going through to cause you to miss your vehicle to destiny.

Favor on the Journey

After arriving in Egypt, Joseph was sold by the Ishmaelites as a slave to an Egyptian officer named Potiphar, but "the Lord was with Joseph." See how God favored Joseph in the land of Egypt:

> *Whatever it takes, God knows how to navigate your life's situation to get you there.*

> *Now Joseph had been taken down to Egypt; and Potiphar, an Egyptian officer of Pharaoh, the captain of the [royal] guard, bought him from the Ishmaelites, who had taken him down there. The LORD was with Joseph, and he [even though a slave] became a successful and prosperous man; and he was in the house of his master, the Egyptian. Now his master saw that the LORD was with him and that the LORD caused all that he did to*

prosper (succeed) in his hand. So Joseph pleased Potiphar and found favor in his sight and he served him as his personal servant. He made Joseph overseer over his house, and he put all that he owned in Joseph's charge.
Genesis 39:1–4, AMP

Despite what the Lord allows you to go through as He transforms you on this journey of preparation, the favor that God has over your life will be undeniable. The favor of God will not only protect you from the enemy as God does His work in you, but this favor will cause God's light to shine on you, causing men to see your good works, which will give you favor with God and man. Potiphar saw that the Lord was with Joseph, and he made him overseer over his entire house and all that he owned, and Joseph became successful and prosperous, even in the valley of testing.

Now just think about it, a slave running around with authority as a supervisor. God was working in two-part harmony using Joseph's position as a slave and servant leader to develop him in humility and leadership. The Lord used Joseph's position as a slave to further develop his character while using his position as the overseer to develop his leadership skills, enhancing his ability to influence, manage, and lead others. Remember, the plan is to develop you in all areas, not to destroy you.

A Dream Deferred, but Not Denied

I recall another of my most trying periods of testing that God allowed me to endure while being developed in the valley. I too had a dream that the Lord had given me, one that revealed elevation and repositioning for my next kingdom assignment, with many prophetic words of confirmation concerning what God was going to do in my life. However, I knew from much experience that God had more developing and grooming to do in me to prepare me for such a task.

As a part of my development process, God allowed an iron fist to come into my life. This iron-fisted mentality would change my life forever. The Word of God puts it like this:

> *As iron sharpens iron, so one person sharpens another.*
> *Proverbs 27:17, NIV*

One of the first things we must learn to do is follow the leader; regardless of your opinion of them, they are the appointed leader. Please remember that even though a person may make it hard to honor them because of certain behaviors, they are still the designated leader, and you must learn to honor their position of leadership, if you plan to succeed.

I learned to do this by humbling myself under the mighty hand of God and submitting to leadership, while continuing to pray for the leader despite the circumstances. As a result, the favor of God was truly upon me. No matter how this iron fist pounded and cut away, I always knew that God was with me and in control of my destiny.

During this time of testing God allowed me to experience many humbling and somewhat emotionally crushing things. First, I was abruptly shifted from my job position and responsibilities as a director, a position that I had successfully held for many years. And I didn't understand why. I was then moved from my larger office that accommodated my assigned staff and the clients we served into a small place of isolation. There, I was distanced from the executive leadership team that I'd always been a part of, as well as the camaraderie of my former team and other coworkers that I had always been so accustomed to. (This was the most difficult for one who is called to deal with people, such as I.) Much of the time I was left alone in the presence of God, praying and hearing from God in a way I'd never experienced before.

I was consistently reassigned from one set of new leadership tasks to another (blessed by God to succeed at them all), which at times was so emotionally draining that I almost gave in to the pressure. Pressure squeezed me in so many ways that my tears no longer felt like water, but they began to feel like oil running down my face. But just as the Lord was with Joseph, the Lord was with me.

The oil of anointing coming from all the pressure I endured produced such a glow in my life that it caused many of my coworkers to comment on the brightness of my countenance in the midst of seemingly unbearable circumstances. This radiant glow encouraged many of my coworkers, who were experiencing similar tests and trials, to remain faithful and walk in their integrity as well. The things that happened to me while in God's school of preparation have now become the things that I teach to others. Know that the dream you have may be deferred in order for God to prepare you, but it will not be denied, and at the appointed time, it will come to pass.

After coming through nearly two years of preparation, I was able to reflect on some of the following key things to relay to others who may be going through a similar process:

The Shifting: Sometimes for God to get us into the position He has ordained for our next kingdom assignment, God has to shift us out of our comfort zone. This can be difficult for those who are creatures of habit and generally resist change. Therefore, God will do it suddenly, without warning or time for you to resist the process.

The Stripping: Sometimes we have many layers of stuff that hinder us from absorbing God's fresh oil of anointing. Therefore, like old furniture before it can be restored, God has to strip the many layers of things that are no longer useful or hinder our growth, sometimes down to the bare bones. Although it is painful and feels shameful for a season, the end result is going to be beautiful.

The Isolation: Sometimes those of you who have a particular leadership call from God on your life can feel very isolated, as God allows you to be separated from the pack to a place where He can speak to your spirit and give you instructions for your next kingdom assignment. However, you must also be aware that this place of isolation can be a stronghold for the enemy and a time the enemy intentionally plots (remember God plans, but Satan plots) to isolate you from others (whether physically, emotionally, or both) in an attempt to reject, disgrace, and discourage you. Satan's goal is to stop you from pursuing your God-ordained purpose, because the enemy knows he has no control over your destiny. Therefore, you must prayerfully stay focused on God's will for your life and obey God, no matter the circumstance.

The Newly Assigned Tasks: At first all of the changes and newly assigned task hurled at you can be frustrating and, like me, may even make you feel like giving up. But this is not the time for giving up; it's the time for learning. You must see yourself as a sponge absorbing every opportunity to learn new tasks and strengthen your skills, because you will need everything that God is equipping you with to excel in your next kingdom assignment. Most people tend to think that kingdom assignments are only in the spiritual realm of work, but God wants to position His people in every area of life from your house to the White House and every place in between. So hold on, because soon it will all work together for your good, in accordance with the purpose that God has for you.

The Moving: There are times when you have simply outgrown (reached maximum benefit) the place where you are. There may be absolutely nothing wrong with the place. It's simply that you've reached your God-intended goal, and God wants to move you to another level or new assignment. One of the struggles with walking in the will of God is others who don't understand what God is doing in your life may try to discourage you from obeying God's will. You must keep moving because one of the worst things you can ever do is overstay your time in anything. Always remember that when your assignment is over or the season has ended, you must move on. If you delay or tarry, the enemy can get an advantage over you and cause all kinds of devastation in your life. But when you know it's God urging you forward, you must continue to move toward God's master plan for you.

Note to Leaders:

The task of blessing and releasing one you've invested much time and energy in can be a difficult thing to do. The mind-set of many pastors or organizational leaders is that these emerging leaders were raised up to enhance the current house or to support your position as a leader. However, like the children God entrusted us to prepare for adulthood and then bless and release to their own life and calling, so it is with those who God has lent to you for a season. You must know when it is time to bless and release those who you have helped to prepare for their kingdom assignment.

God Has a Master Plan

It has been my experience that a lot of leaders become frustrated or even angry with those leaders whose time has come to be released to go their next kingdom assignment. Frustration can cause leaders to push the person out or force them to break out instead of being blessed and released with dignity and honor for both the leader and the one being called by God. What a great honor and a blessing it is to have a part in preparing and releasing someone for their next kingdom assignment. Remember, as you bless and release leaders called by God, God will bless other leaders to emerge to be a blessing and support in the house or the organization.

Thankfully, I was released with honors, tears, and a great celebration from my job assignment (even honored by the iron fist), after enduring the process of growth and development for my next kingdom assignment. I now see very clearly, after coming out of the dark room of development, that God actually allowed that iron fist into my life to sharpen me as God prepared me for the greater work.

And through it all, much like Joseph, God blessed me with divine favor as I remained faithful and walked in personal integrity, even in the midst of adversity. I truly learned much through the awesome task of humbling myself under the mighty hand of God. If you humble yourself, He will exalt you in due season (God's appointed time). And after this you will be prepared and ready for your next kingdom assignment.

Humble yourselves therefore under the mighty hand of God, that he may exalt you in due time: casting all your care upon him; for he careth for you.
1 Peter 5:6–7, KJV

To say that I didn't experience pain or wonder why I had to go through this wouldn't be the truth, because it was a very painful and sometimes demeaning, yet humbling process. But somehow I always knew it wasn't meant to destroy me, but to prepare me. I learned how to cast my cares upon the Lord, knowing He cares for me. I learned to exercise true forgiveness, knowing that all of this would someday work together for my good. God has manifested His plan for my life in so many ways that it would take another book to tell it all. But trust me, I learned things through this process that were so vital to my destiny, and I can now say that it was worth every step of the journey because a better version me was waiting on the other side.

Joseph's Ultimate Test

Remember I told you that the devil is relentless. Joseph worked very hard to build his character and establish trust with his master and among his master's household, then he was tested to the maximum.

Let's look at the enemy's relentless pursuit of Joseph:

> **"I learned how to cast my cares upon the Lord, knowing He cares for me."**

Now Joseph was handsome and attractive in form and appearance. Then after a time his master's wife looked at Joseph with desire, and she said, "Lie with me." But he refused. And so it was that she spoke to Joseph [persistently] day after day, but he did not listen to her [plea] to lie beside her or be with her. Then it happened one day that Joseph went into the house to attend to his duties, and none of the men of

the household was there in the house. She caught Joseph by his [outer] robe, saying, "Lie with me!" But he left his robe in her hand and ran, and got outside [the house.] Then she told her husband the same story, saying, "The Hebrew servant, whom you brought among us, came to me to mock and insult me; then as soon as I raised my voice and screamed, he left his robe with me and ran outside [the house]." And when Joseph's master heard the words of his wife, saying, "This is the way your servant treated me," his anger burned. So Joseph's master took him and put him in the prison, a place where the king's prisoners were confined; so he was there in the prison.
Genesis 39:6–8, 10–12, 17–20, AMP

How awful Joseph must have felt, not just because Mrs. Potiphar lied, accusing him of attempted rape, but more because the master for whom he had worked so hard to honor with his character and integrity has now lost faith and trust in him. Potiphar believed this terrible lie against him and threw him into prison (a place of confinement).

Wow, what a very difficult accusation to swallow. Some of the greatest tricks of the enemy is to lie on you, destroy your character in the eyes of others, discourage you, and imprison you one way or another (whether behind confined walls in the natural or in your mind). He knows if he can confine your emotions and thoughts and pull you away from what God is saying and doing, then he can defeat you. But even in all this, let's see what the scripture says concerning Joseph:

But the LORD was with Joseph and extended lovingkindness to him, and gave him favor in the sight of the warden. The warden committed to Joseph's care (management) all the prisoners who were in the pris-

> *on; so that whatever was done there, he was in charge of it. The warden paid no attention to anything that was in Joseph's care because the LORD was with him; whatever Joseph did, the LORD made to prosper.*
>
> Genesis 39:21-23, AMP

Favor in the Prison

Right about now, I am jumping for joy because there is nobody like the Lord! Just when you think there's somewhere the enemy can take you that the Lord will not go with you, look again. The Lord was with Joseph, even in the prison. If you find yourself behind prison walls of any kind, go ahead and rejoice in knowing that there's nowhere you can go that the Lord will not be with you, especially when He has a master plan for your life. If that's the place designed to build your character and to prepare you for your kingdom assignment, then so be it. Remember, Joseph not only found favor with God behind these prison walls, but he also found favor with the warden, who put Joseph in charge of everything in the prison because he knew that the Lord was with Joseph. And whatever Joseph did, the Lord made it to prosper.

Your Gift Will Make Room for You

> *A man's gift makes room for him, and brings him before great men.*
>
> Proverbs 18:16, NKJV

The Lord knows when it's time to reveal His master plan for your life. After two full years of being in prison, God unveiled His master plan for Joseph through a sequence of events. Joseph's gift as a dream interpreter (after being perfected by God) was about to be on display before many and launch him into his destiny. After being called upon to interpret the dreams of two of the king's officials (the butler and the baker) with accuracy, Joseph's gift of interpretation made room for him and set him before the king to interpret his disturbing dream.

> *Then Pharaoh sent and called for Joseph, and they hurriedly brought him out of the dungeon; and when Joseph shaved himself and changed his clothes [making himself presentable], he came to Pharaoh. Pharaoh said to Joseph, "I have dreamed a dream, and there is no one who can interpret it; and I have heard it said about you that you can understand a dream and interpret it." Joseph answered Pharaoh, "It is not in me [to interpret the dream]; God [not I] will give Pharaoh a favorable answer [through me]."*
> *Genesis 41:14–16, AMP*

We can see from Joseph's reply to Pharaoh that he had matured and learned much on his journey. Joseph now relied on God to lead him with his gift as a dreamer and to interpret Pharaoh's dreams, and he gave God the glory for the answer concerning the dream. He no longer pranced around blurting out dreams or interpretations without consulting God. What a transformation from the young immature dreamer to the gifted servant leader developed by God.

God's Master Plan Revealed

God used Joseph to let Pharaoh know that very quickly his dream would come to pass. He told him there would be seven years of abundant crop growth in which the land would be greatly blessed, followed by seven years of famine and hunger so devastating that the previous years of abundance would soon be forgotten. However, God also gave Joseph wisdom and a master plan that he unfolded to Pharaoh for saving the people, which involved creating a food bank and financial reserve system (see Genesis 41:29–31; 33–36).

Remember, God will not only use our spiritual gifts and talents, but He will also use our natural gifts and talents to accomplish His purpose. Joseph was more than just a prophetic dream interpreter; he had many natural gifts and talents that were valuable for his kingdom assignment.

Joseph advised Pharaoh that this new government reserve system should be under a leader with wisdom and discernment, and this leader should be set in charge over the land as governor under Pharaoh. Joseph also told Pharaoh that the governor would need a team of officials to oversee the project. Watch how Pharaoh responded to God's Master Plan:

> *So Pharaoh said to his servants, "Can we find a man like this [a man equal to Joseph], in whom is the divine spirit [of God]?" Then Pharaoh said to Joseph, "Since [your] God has shown you all this, there is no one as discerning and clear-headed and wise as you are. You shall have charge over my house, and all my people shall be governed according to your word and pay respect [to you with reverence, submission, and obedience]; only in [matters of] the throne will I be greater than you [in Egypt]." Then Pharaoh said to Joseph, "See, I have set you [in charge] over all the land of Egypt."*
>
> *Genesis 41:38–41*

God Has a Master Plan

I love it when God orchestrates a plan and we can plainly see it unfold according to His method, His timing, and His purpose, which are always in harmony pertaining to His master plan. From the Lord, Joseph learned much traveling through God's school of preparation. Schooling not only prepared this little dreamer to be a leader over his family, but also to be governor over a nation. God developed many notable qualities and character traits in Joseph's life, including wisdom, discernment, trustworthiness, humility, respect, reverence, obedience, vision, leadership skills, organizational skills, financial management skills, and the ability to follow a leader.

Now can you recognize what God is trying to develop in you? Please remember that just because your dream is deferred, it does not mean that it is not going to come to pass.

Elevated by God

I know many who are called by God believe that they are ready to leap tall buildings in a single bound. However, until you understand God's process of development for your life, you will continue to be grounded, never truly being elevated by God to effectively fulfill your purpose.

Pharaoh and some of his officials watched Joseph and observed the Lord's special anointing for leadership upon his life. Joseph didn't have any fancy educational degrees or titles, but he passed the test of humility and submission and graduated from God's school of preparation with the master's degree of readiness—an honorable degree that will open doors of opportunity that no man can shut. Joseph was elevated by God from the pit to the palace, a miraculous door that no man could shut (Revelation 3:8).

For some, your journey may not take as much as it took for Joseph, while for others it may take more. But whatever it takes, remember Jesus is with you, and He has a master plan for your life. Humility and submission are the keys that unlock the doors. If you remain faithful and willing to learn in God's school of preparation, there is an elevation that awaits you, and you too will come out a better you, ready to fulfill your kingdom assignment after this.

Kingdom Notes

After reading chapter 7, God Has a Master Plan for You, let's pause and take a few kingdom notes.

1. Do you have knowledge of the call of God that is upon your life or knowledge of your next kingdom assignment? If so, write it down.

2. While reading about Joseph's experience of being thrown into the pit until his elevation into the palace, what similarities do you recognize concerning your personal journey through the school of preparation?

3. What is the vehicle (circumstance) God is using to test you and transport you to your appointed destination?

4. Do you know the gift(s) inside of you that will bring you before great men? If so, explain.

5. Check off some of the areas you recognize that God needs to perfect in you:

___Wisdom   ___ Discernment   ___ Trust

God Has a Master Plan

___ Honesty ___ Integrity ___ Respect

___ Obedience ___ Vengeance ___ Prayer

___ Humility ___ Temperance ___ Reverence

___ Submission ___ Forgiveness ___ Leadership skills

___ Recognizing and operating in my gift ___ Faith

Let's Pray

Father, in the name of Jesus, thank You for selecting me to be a chosen vessel that You are forming and making into a vessel of honor, fit for Your use. Lord, I humble myself before You, asking You to order my steps. Please help me to understand and acknowledge Your master plan for my life. Please help me to let go and let You be Lord of my life. Please help me to shed any bitterness or anger that has taken hold of me because of the preparation process. Lord, make me an effective instrument for Your glory, ready for my kingdom assignment. Amen!

Chapter Eight

After This

After you have suffered for a little while, the God of all grace [who imparts His blessing and favor], who called you to His own eternal glory in Christ, will Himself complete, confirm, strengthen, and establish you [making you what you ought to be].
—1 Peter 5:10, AMP

While traveling through this journey of preparation, it may seem like an endless amount of time passes as you endure hardness as a good soldier equipped for your kingdom assignment. But in actuality, on God's timetable of preparation, He deems it as only a little while. Then, after you've suffered for a little while, completing your individual lesson plan, the God of all grace who distributes His blessings and favor and called us for His glory in Christ Jesus will Himself equip you in every area of readiness. Here's what He will do:

- Complete you: After the process is over, you will be

complete (whole) in Him with nothing missing or lacking in your life (James 1:4).

- Confirm you: After the process is over, you will be affirmed by God and declared qualified regardless of what man might try to say to disqualify you (2 Corinthians 1:20–22).

- Strengthen you: After the process is over, you will be strong in the Lord and in the power of His might (Ephesian 6:10).

- Establish you: After the process is over, you will no longer be tossed about by every wind or doctrine, but you will be "steadfast, immovable always abounding in the work of the Lord, knowing that your labor is not in vain in the Lord" (1 Corinthians 15:58).

- Making you what you ought to be: After the process is over, you will be who God called you to be and walk according to His plan for your life (Jeremiah 29:11).

No Time for Bitterness, Anger, or Painful Remembrances

As we come to the climax of Joseph's story, we see the essence and character of a man who has been developed by God. During his journey, Joseph could've justified being bitter toward a lot of different people and difficult circumstances. However, he didn't allow bitterness, resentment, unforgiveness, anger, or even the smell of smoke from the refining fire to attach itself to him. Therefore, we see him being promoted by God into a position of authority, trust, and leadership, equipped to lead the nations.

Here are the four main reasons Joseph was able to avoid

a life of bitterness and anger toward the people and/or circumstances that caused him so much hurt and pain during his journey of preparation:

1. He always knew (as revealed to him in his dreams) that God had a master plan for his life. He always recognized God's favor upon his life even through rejection, emotional family abuse, being stripped of his beloved garment (outward blessings), attempted murder upon his life, being thrown in a slimy dark pit, separation from his family, loneliness in a strange land, attempts to assassinate his character, rejection by his trusted leader, innocently thrown into prison, the pain of broken promises, and so much more. God's favor continually made him the head and not the tail in every situation; therefore, he always honored God and walked with integrity.

As a result hear what the Lord promises:

The Lord will make you the head, not the tail. If you pay attention to the commands of the Lord your God that I give you this day and carefully follow them, you will always be at the top, never at the bottom.
Deuteronomy 28:13, NIV

2. After coming through his tests and trials, he never failed to recognize that his gifts were from God, and despite the circumstances, his gifts would always make room for him.

3. With time, he finally understood that God was operating through his circumstances and preparing him for a greater assignment. Therefore, he knew that his battle was not against flesh and blood (those used by the

enemy to hurt him), but against spiritual wickedness in high places that didn't want to see him arrive at his God-assigned destination (Ephesians 6:12).

4. He kept a heart of forgiveness knowing that what the devil meant for evil, God was going to use for his good to save many lives.

A True Heart of Forgiveness

"Please come closer to me," Joseph asked his brothers. The same brothers who'd hated him, left him to die in the pit, and sold him to strangers. Joseph forgave all those who sinned against him.

One true test of forgiveness is if you can comfortably be in the presence of your offenders and invite them to come close to you again. Though in some circumstances this may not always be possible, Joseph really loved his brothers and understood that God had a purpose for all that he'd endured. He wanted his brothers to see the love of God in him and to understand the true purpose of his journey to Egypt. Joseph embraced his brothers and let them know that he was indeed their brother Joseph, whom they had sold into Egypt, and they should not be sad or distressed. He let them know that they were all a part of God's master plan. Listen as Joseph forgivingly comforts his brothers:

> *One true test of forgiveness is if you can comfortably be in the presence of your offenders...*

> Now do not be distressed or angry with yourselves because you sold me here, for God sent me ahead of you to

save life and preserve our family.

Genesis 45:5, AMP

Once Joseph clearly understood his purpose and what God was doing in his life by sending him ahead to Egypt to save lives and preserve his family, God touched his heart, and he let go of the pain caused along his journey and forgave all those who had caused such hurt and pain. True forgiveness is a vital part of our lesson plan from God, who teaches us the importance of releasing others from our pain, resentment, or silent emotional punishment toward them. And if we don't forgive others who sin against us, then our heavenly Father will not forgive us when we sin (Matthew 6:14–15, NIV).

You must not allow the test and trials of your life's journey to make you bitter and angry at people or the circumstances you've endured. But rather embrace the lessons you've learned, forgive those who have hurt you, and grow on from here. After the test is over, the blessings of being called and equipped by God will far outweigh anything you have gone through.

After This, Everything Connected to You Shall Be Blessed

After Joseph lovingly made himself known to his brothers, he not only forgave and embraced them, but he also summoned his entire family to come to the land of blessings to be with him. Hear what Joseph said:

> *Hurry and go up to my father, and tell him, "Your son Joseph says this to you: 'God has made me lord of all Egypt; come down to me, do not delay. You shall live in the land of Goshen [the best pasture land of Egypt], and you shall*

> *be close to me—you and your children and your grandchildren, your flocks and your herds and all you have. There I will provide for you and sustain you, so that you and your household and all that are yours may not become impoverished, for there are still five years of famine to come."*
>
> Genesis 45:9–11, AMP

Just look how God brought Joseph into the place of abundance to bless and sustain his entire family. Once you have completed God's school of preparation, you too will be blessed and positioned in a place not only to be blessed, but to be a blessing to all that are connected. When Pharaoh heard that Joseph had been reunited with his family, he also sanctioned a blessing upon Joseph's family because he favored Joseph. Hear what Pharaoh declared:

> *Then Pharaoh said to Joseph, "Tell your brothers, 'Do this: load your animals and return to the land of Canaan [without delay], and get your father and your households and come to me. I will give you the best of the land of Egypt, and you will eat the fat (the finest produce) of the land."*
>
> Genesis 45:16–18, AMP

You Shall Eat the Fat of the Land

What blessings are in store for you and all who are connected to you once you come through the night season of preparation. God's best (the fat of the land) is reserved for all who yield to the process and allow God to prepare you for your next kingdom assignment. All will know that you have been called and chosen by God as you are positioned in the place of blessing *after this*.

Epilogue

Job's story of tragedy, tests and trials, triumph, and victory is one that may still baffle many to this day. But what comes out of his very difficult night season is this: The Lord was always with Job and had a master plan for his life. The enemy had to get permission from God to bypass the protective hedge that surrounded Job's life and touch all that belonged to him. And even then, there was only so far that the enemy was allowed to go before God would ring the bell (stop the fight) and step in to restore Job. What joy and confidence it is in knowing that ultimately in the end we win. It will be a victory that will reward us with a double portion of blessings for all that we've gone through for God. And most importantly, like Job, we will get to know God in a way we have never known him before.

Joseph was just seventeen years old when God gave him a powerful dream concerning his kingdom assignment. It was an assignment so powerful that it would take years of teaching in the God's school of preparation before the dream would come to fulfillment. His individual lesson plan of preparation would include some very difficult lessons to be learned, as God molded, shaped, and prepared him, equipping him with all that he would need to become not only the leader of his family, but also the governor of a nation.

The Bible speaks of many in the Hall of Faith, who withstood many test and trials as they traveled through their various night seasons to fulfill their kingdom assignments, of whom the world was not worthy (Hebrews 11). Yet according to verses 39–40, even they didn't receive all the promises that God has in store for us who prevail. The Bible declares that the world is anxiously awaiting "the manifestation of the sons of God"(Romans 8:19) the day when those who've been quality tested and prepared by God are ready to be released to effectively fulfill their God-ordained purpose in the earth.

Whether you realize it or not, God's people are the answer to the world's crisis today as we emerge ready to fulfill our kingdom assignments. Those who have passed the test of preparation and gained wisdom from the journey will be able to minister with the faith that God has the power to transform or strengthen any life, regardless of the circumstances. Your transformed life will have the ability to "reproduce" others for the kingdom of God, and together we can defeat the power of the enemy that plagues the world today.

Our Lord and Savior Jesus Christ was the answer to the crisis of sin that plagued us all. His assignment to save mankind was not an easy journey. Yet, despite the difficulties of His night season, Jesus endured the process, dying on the cross to save mankind, and because of His death, burial, and

Epilogue

resurrection, He is the "door" that gives us access to God the Father (John 14:6). Therefore, He is now seated at the right hand of God, on the throne as our Lord and King forever. Listen as the Word of God gives us the example we are to follow:

> *Therefore let us also, seeing we are compassed about with so great a cloud of witnesses, lay aside every weight, and the sin which doth so easily beset us, and let us run with patience the race that is set before us, looking unto Jesus the author and perfecter of our faith, who for the joy that was set before him endured the cross, despising shame, and hath sat down at the right hand of the throne of God.*
>
> Hebrews 12:1-2, ASV

As one who has been called and equipped by the Lord for a God-ordained purpose, I know firsthand how God will use the circumstances of your life (whether good or bad) to prepare you for your kingdom assignment. While traveling through my personal journey of preparation, the enemy formed many weapons that were designed to destroy me, but God blocked every weapon sent to abolish my purpose (Isaiah 54:17). There were even times that I tried to jump off of the potter's wheel of preparation, but praise God He loved me enough to catch me in midair and put me back on the wheel. Spinning me round by round, as He touched every area of my life, pruning me to remove any hindrances that would prevent me from being a vessel of honor prepared for the Master's use. Timothy puts it this way:

> *If a man therefore purge himself from these, he shall be a vessel unto honour, sanctified, and meet [ready] for the master's use, and prepared unto every good work.*
>
> 2 Timothy 2:21, KJV

After This

I pray that the transparency of my personal journey, which included some excruciating pain, powerful lessons for growth and development, compassionate healing, forgiveness, and triumphant victories during my night season of preparation, will be the tool needed to dig you out of the rut that hinders you from moving through your season of preparation with grace, integrity, and determination to be ready for your next kingdom assignment.

Let's take notes from the tragedy suffered by the Children of Israel, who turned an eleven-day journey into forty years of wandering in the wilderness. Many of them died in the wilderness and never reached the reward waiting in the Promise Land all because of their disobedience, pride, unbelief, and the refusal to change, even though God was always with them, guiding them and working miracles on their behalf. Let's not prolong the the journey of preparation and miss the promises of God by making some of the same mistakes.

I am not by any means saying that the journey will be easy (some of us could sing the Richard White song "I'm Glad I Don't Look Like What I've Been Through), but like the old saints, I didn't wait until the battle was over to rejoice; I kept praising God right in the midst of the storm. I learned to speak "victory" during the test, and I can now say I am grateful for every step of my journey. What an awesome God we serve!

It's my hope that every chosen vessel will realize, as did Job, Joseph, the many patriarchs, and even me, that the lessons were never meant to destroy you, but rather to strengthen and prepare you for your kingdom assignment. And though weeping may endure for a night season, if you can just hold out until the morning (God's appointed time of breakthrough), joy and blessings await you after this.

Epilogue

For his anger endureth but a moment; in his favour is life: weeping may endure for a night [season], but joy cometh in the morning.

Psalm 30:5, KJV

Blessings and Big Hugs, Dr. D.

About the Author

Dr. Madelyne Douglas has been an ordained minister of the gospel of Jesus Christ since 1974. "Dr. D.," as she is fondly known by many, has been a keynote speaker and motivational facilitator at many revivals, women's retreats, youth programs, educational workshops, and community outreach programs. Dr. Douglas has been a youth director and trainer for over thirty-five years in the greater Kansas City area, working with youth from all walks of life. She has trained youth leaders at Niles Home for Children, various schools, churches of all denominations, and various other community organizations. Dr. Douglas is a playwright and has written, directed, and performed several plays in the greater Kansas City area and in various cities throughout the country. Dr. Douglas served as the director of residential services of Niles Home for Children as well as other key senior management positions, retiring after twenty-one years of service.

In 2000, Dr. Douglas received her doctorate in counseling and in christian education and administration from Faith Bible College. In 2001, Dr. Douglas received board certification as a marriage and family christian therapist with the American Society of Christian Therapists. Dr. Douglas is currently an instructor at Faith Bible College, teaching Crisis Counseling I and II, and is a member of the college advisory board. Dr. Douglas received her doctorate degree in theology from Faith Bible College in 2003. Dr. Douglas was chosen as one of the progressive women in leadership for the state of Missouri and is a graduate of the Greater Missouri Leadership Challenge, class of 2005. After graduating from the program, Dr. Douglas served for many years as a regional coordinator for Greater Missouri Leadership Challenge. Dr. Douglas is an alumni member of the board of directors for Habitat for Humanity. In 2015, Dr. Douglas received her state certification as a Missouri Recovery Support Specialist, working with families who are recovering from substance use and addictions.

Dr. Madelyne Douglas is the founder of the Glory Train Community Mobile Ministry, a community ministry that is ordained by God to reach the hurting and the lost, assisting them back to the safety of the church and the loving arm of Jesus Christ. Dr. Douglas is currently an associate pastor at the Victory Temple Christian Life Center, under the leadership of Bishop Keith and Pastor Latonya Tribitt. Dr. Douglas, along with her late husband, Larry Douglas Sr. are the proud parents of Annita and Larry Jr. and the proud grandparents of six beautiful grandchildren: Melvin, Naesion, Marshawn, Delvin, Larry (L.J.) III, and Sierra.

To God be the glory!

You can see Dr. D on her FB Live Show "*In the Kitchen with Dr. D.*" Join her membership list for teachings and updates.

Connect with Dr. D

 @Dr.DMinistries

 dr.mrd7@gmail.com

 MyAfterThis.com

MORE BOOKS FROM EAR TO HEAR PUBLISHING & SHE PROCLAIMS IMPRINT

Inner Beauty: Goodbye Self-Rejection and Hello Self-Love Beyond the Mirror by Author Isabel Perez-McCoy

Dear Woman: Losing hope in the midst of chronic pain and finding it again (A memoir) by Author Chavos Buycks

Do you feel called to write a book? If the answer is yes, then Ear To Hear Publishing might be able to help you. Visit our website for more information to complete the publishing assessment and get connected with our writer's group.

www.EartoHearBooks.com

www.ingramcontent.com/pod-product-compliance
Lightning Source LLC
Chambersburg PA
CBHW050557300426
44112CB00013B/1964